Leadership and the Cross

A 52-WEEK DEVOTIONAL FOR LEADERS

Dr. Chase Raymond

Leadership and the Cross

Leadership and the Cross
© Chase J. Raymond 2025

Title: *Leadership and the Cross: A 52-Week Devotional for Leaders*
ISBN: 979-8-90148-712-9

All rights reserved. No portion of this book may be reproduced, stored in a retrieval system, or transmitted in any form or by any means; electronic, mechanical, photocopy, recording, scanning, or other except for brief quotations in critical reviews or articles, without the prior written permission of the publisher.

All devotional reflections, stories, and commentary are original works of the author. Any resemblance to real persons or published materials is purely coincidental or used with permission.

Unless otherwise noted, Scripture quotations are from the Holy Bible, New International Version®, NIV®. Copyright © 1973, 1978, 1984, 2011 by Biblica, Inc. The "NIV" and "New International Version" are trademarks registered in the United States Patent and Trademark Office by Biblica, Inc.®

Published by Staton House

www.timeforleadership.com

Acknowledgments

This devotional is the fruit of several years of prayer, study, and the gracious influence of those supporting me along the way. I am deeply grateful to those who have walked alongside me and demonstrated what Christlike leadership looks like in action.

To Dr. Cathy Hutchings-Wedel, a mentor and friend, thank you for being a faithful witness for Jesus and for continually encouraging me to write this devotional.

I would also like to acknowledge my family. Your unwavering love, encouragement, and prayers have been the quiet strength in everything I do, including every word on these pages.

Finally, I give all glory to Jesus Christ, who is the ultimate example of true leadership, and whose Spirit empowers us to live out these principles daily.

To all leaders…

Let nothing be done through selfish ambition or conceit, but in lowliness of mind let each esteem others better than himself. Let each of you look not only to his own interests, but also to the interests of others. Let this mind be in you which was also in Christ Jesus
Philippians 2:3-5

Introduction

Leadership is more than titles, positions, or power. At its core, leadership is influence rooted in character. The Bible offers lessons on leadership that remain as relevant today as they were thousands of years ago. From Moses guiding Israel through the wilderness to Esther's courage before a king to Jesus washing His disciples' feet, Scripture shows that leadership is not about self-promotion but about serving others and honoring God.

Designed for leaders, this devotional equips you to guide your team or organization by integrating Christian principles with proven leadership theory. Further this devotional follows the *C.R.O.S.S. Leadership Model*, which is a faith-based framework that is designed to shape leaders through five core principles:

Character: Leading with integrity and authenticity, even when no one is watching.

Responsibility: Owning actions, decisions, and their impact on others.

Obedience: Aligning leadership with God's guidance rather than personal ambition.

Service: Placing the needs of others above self-interest and leading with humility.

© Chase Raymond 2025

Sacrifice: Willingness to give up comfort, recognition, or advantage for a greater purpose.

Together, these principles form a Christ-centered approach to leadership; one that transforms influence into impact and authority into stewardship.

Over the next 52 weeks, you will work through 10 core areas of leadership, including strategic thinking, decision making, problem solving, communication, trust building, organizational change, conflict management, ethics, teamwork, and applying modern leadership approaches. Together, these weekly devotions are designed to help you grow as a leader who not only makes wise decisions but also embodies the way of the cross in daily life.

Leadership is much like a pebble thrown into a pond, as its impact ripples outward, touching everything around it. Those ripples can bring life and renewal, or they can stir confusion and harm. I intended this devotional to send forth ripples that are positive, healing, and far-reaching, inspiring leaders to influence others with grace, integrity, and purpose. I pray these pages serve as a steady companion on your leadership journey, always pointing you to the ultimate model of leadership found at the cross of Christ.

How to Use This Devotional

This devotional is structured to guide you through an entire year of Christlike leadership development. Here's how each week is designed:

- **Weekly Leadership Topic:** This 52-week devotional is divided into ten distinct themes, each exploring a core challenge or question faced by leaders. Every five weeks introduces a new subject such as strategic thinking, communication, trust-building, the leader's calling, organizational change, problem-solving and decision-making, conflict management, motivating your team, the fear of taking the lead, and ethical leadership. Each theme is addressed through five weekly devotionals that help leaders reflect deeply, apply biblical truth, and align their leadership with Christ-centered values. These five-week blocks provide consistent encouragement, practical insight, and spiritual grounding for the unique demands of leadership.

- **Scripture:** Begin with God's Word. Read each scripture slowly, and ask the Holy Spirit to open your heart to what He wants to reveal.

- **Leadership Wisdom for the Christian Leader:** Each section connects Scripture to the realities of organizational leadership, providing clear, actionable guidance shaped by conviction, character, and faith.

- **Weekly Practice in Faith**: Apply the week's principle through specific, doable actions in your leadership, work, or relationships.

- **Reflection:** Each week use the reflection as time to consider what God is revealing about leadership in their own life. We suggest using a simple journal, such as the *Leadership and the Cross Leadership Journal* to process your thoughts and emotions, and record God's work in your life. This practice creates a tangible record of your spiritual journey, helps you remember answered prayers, and allows you to see how you have grown as a leader over time.

- **Weekly Prayer:** Use the guided weekly prayer to bring your leadership journey before God.

Leadership and the Cross

STRATEGIC THINKING

Weeks 1 - 5

Strategic thinking is an essential skill that leaders must have to make informed decisions. For Christians, it is more than analysis; it is choosing a course of action that aligns with Scripture, character, and mission when pressure is high and outcomes are uncertain. Over the next five weeks you will practice grounding choices in character and wisdom, acting with courage, widening perspective through collaboration, and remaining faithful in difficult seasons. As a leader, your goal is to make Christ-centered choices that advance the mission and care for the people you lead.

WEEK 1

Develop Character Before Strategy

"And David shepherded them with integrity of heart;

with skillful hands he led them"

Psalm 78:72 (NIV)

Leadership often reveals itself most clearly in difficult moments rather than in carefully planned strategies. The challenges, pressures, and trials we face are rarely accidental. God often uses these situations to test our hearts, refine our faith, and shape who we are beneath the surface. Throughout Scripture, we see leaders whose lasting impact was rooted not in their brilliance, but in their character.

Moses did not earn his influence through strategy alone. His authority flowed from humility and obedience. Esther's courage before the king was not merely political instinct; it was trust in God's timing and sovereignty. And David, long before his crown, tended sheep with faithfulness and integrity. His leadership was formed in obscurity before it was ever displayed in authority. These stories remind us that strategy is only as strong as the character beneath it.

As this journey begins, we are challenged to reflect on what anchors our leadership. Biblical leadership does not start with position or plans. It begins with alignment. When our decisions flow from a heart shaped by God, leadership becomes not only effective, but faithful. Skillful hands matter, but only when they are guided by an integrity shaped heart.

Leadership Wisdom for the Christian Leader

In many organizations, leaders regularly face strategic choices that pit short-term financial gains against long-term values and culture. Under pressure from shifting markets and shareholder expectations, it can be tempting to pursue options that quickly boost profits, even when they involve cutting corners, downsizing loyal teams, or eroding long-held ethical commitments. When organizations choose instead to slow down, broaden input, and seek value-aligned alternatives, they may delay immediate results but often preserve trust, reinforce a values-based culture, and position themselves for more durable success. Leading with "integrity of heart" means strategy is anchored in what is right, not only in what is profitable or efficient, so that financial decisions remain accountable to deeper moral commitments.

These patterns highlight a broader leadership lesson: strategic decision-making is not only about technical sophistication or clever analysis, but about how consistently organizational choices reflect core values and purpose. When leaders treat strategy as an expression of character, both at the organizational level and individual level, they signal that people, integrity, and long-term relationships matter as much as quarterly metrics. In this sense, "integrity of heart" becomes the inner compass that guides "skillful hands," ensuring that even the most complex plans and interventions serve what is just, wise, and life-giving for the community. Over time, this stance can become a defining organizational asset, attracting committed talent, strengthening partnerships, and sustaining credibility even in turbulent environments.

Weekly Practice in Faith

This week, identify one important decision you are facing. Instead of approaching it purely as a problem to solve, bring it before God each day in prayer. Ask Him to search your motives, refine your intentions, and align your plans with His purposes. Pay attention not only to what you decide, but to what this process reveals about your heart.

Time for Reflection

David's leadership was shaped long before he sat on a throne. His strength did not rest solely in his ability to plan or execute. It was rooted in the integrity that guided his choices and his surrender to God's direction.

Take time to reflect. Is your leadership built primarily on skill and strategy, or is it grounded in character? Are you seeking God to shape your heart as intentionally as you seek His guidance for your plans? Ask Him to reveal where your character needs strengthening so that your leadership flows from who you are, not just what you do.

Weekly Prayer

God, strengthen my character this week. When I am faced with choices, help me pause and listen for Your wisdom. Remind me that strategy without You is hollow. May I lead with a heart that reflects You; in truth, humility, and conviction. Amen.

WEEK 2

Lead with Godly Wisdom

"Where there is no guidance, a people falls,

but in an abundance of counselors there is safety"

Proverbs 11:14 (NIV)

Being a leader is rarely simple. Leadership is filled with decisions, competing priorities, unresolved tensions, and people who study not only your choices but your reactions. In those moments, leaders often feel pressure to appear certain even when they feel anything but. Yet one of the greatest strengths of leadership is knowing when to stop relying solely on yourself and turn to God for wisdom.

Scripture reminds us in Proverbs 20:18 and James 1:5 that wise plans come through counsel and that God gives wisdom generously when we ask. We see this lived out clearly in the life of Moses. Overwhelmed by the responsibility of leading an entire nation, Moses attempted to carry the full burden alone. He listened to every case, managed every dispute, and made every decision. Exhaustion followed. The people grew restless. The system began to strain.

Then Jethro, his father in law, stepped in with wisdom and courage. He spoke a hard truth: what Moses was doing was unsustainable. He urged him to delegate and to trust others with responsibility. Moses could have resisted, clinging to control or pride. Instead, he listened, adjusted, and grew. His willingness to receive counsel strengthened both his leadership and the health of the people.

This pattern reflects the wisdom of Proverbs 11:14, where Scripture teaches that without guidance, people fall, but with many counselors, there is safety. God never designed leadership to be carried alone. Lone ranger leadership may look strong, but it often leads to burnout and blind spots. Godly leadership is shared, sharpened, and sustained through the voices He places around us. Asking for help is not weakness. It is an act of wisdom.

Leadership Wisdom for the Christian Leader

Leaders often face decisions that look simple when viewed only through financial reports or strategic projections. Metrics can tell part of the story, but they rarely reveal the human impact or the long-term consequences that come from acting too quickly. Proverbs 11:14 teaches us that without guidance people fall, and this applies directly to leadership choices that carry weight. Wise leaders slow down, gather counsel, and listen to the voices that are easy to overlook. This includes employees closest to the work, community partners, and those who will feel the effects of the decision long after the spreadsheets are updated.

An abundance of counselors brings safety because it widens a leader's understanding and reduces blind spots. Seeking diverse perspectives is not a sign of insecurity but a sign of maturity. It protects the mission, keeps leaders grounded in values, and often uncovers solutions that balance stewardship with compassion. In a world that rewards speed and efficiency, the strongest leaders are the ones who choose wisdom over haste. They understand that good guidance is not a delay but a safeguard, and that decisions grounded in counsel build trust that lasts.

Weekly Practice in Faith

This week, identify one decision that feels heavy or uncertain. Instead of carrying it alone, intentionally seek input from at least one trusted mentor, colleague, or advisor. As you listen, ask God to quiet your heart and sharpen your discernment. Release the pressure to have every answer. Wisdom often emerges when humility leads and pride steps aside.

Time for Reflection

Godly leadership is never meant to be isolated leadership. Wise leaders recognize that their perspective is limited and that God often speaks through others. Reflect on your leadership posture. Do you tend to withdraw or carry pressure alone when facing difficult decisions? Or do you invite others into the process?

Wisdom is not simply knowing what to do. It is being willing to listen, to weigh counsel, and to trust that God can guide you through the voices He places around you. Ask God to reveal where you need to open your leadership to wise voices rather than relying only on your own instincts.

Weekly Prayer

Father, thank You for your wisdom and your guidance. I am grateful to you for surrounding me with wise counselors and mentors. Give me humility to listen, patience to weigh advice, and courage to act in ways that honor You. Amen.

WEEK 3

Lead with Courage and Conviction

"Have I not commanded you? Be strong and courageous. Do not be afraid; do not be discouraged, for the Lord your God will be with you wherever you go."

Joshua 1:9 (NIV)

As leaders, we are often asked to make decisions that are unpopular, uncomfortable, and costly. There are moments when you must speak while others remain silent, move forward when direction feels unclear, or hold your ground when compromise seems easier. In those moments, leadership demands more than a plan. It requires courage and conviction.

Courage is not the absence of fear. It is the decision to move forward despite it. Conviction is the inner strength to remain anchored in truth, even when that truth brings resistance. Together, they form the backbone of godly leadership, especially when the pressure is high and the outcome is uncertain.

Scripture gives us a powerful example of this in the life of Daniel. Taken from his homeland and placed in a culture opposed to his faith, Daniel faced constant pressure to conform. Yet he chose obedience again and again. He refused to compromise his values at the king's table. He continued to pray openly when it became illegal. His leadership was not reactive or driven by convenience. It was rooted in a deep commitment to God.

Strategic thinking alone is not enough. Leadership also requires the courage to act on what is right, not just what is safe or popular. Followers of Christ are called to lead with conviction that risks comfort, reputation, and certainty for the sake of truth. That kind of leadership may not always be celebrated in the moment, but it carries eternal weight.

This week, consider where fear may be quieting your voice or softening your resolve. God does not only call you to lead. He equips you to lead courageously. When your courage is grounded in conviction, your leadership leaves a mark that stretches beyond the moment and points others toward faithfulness.

Leadership Wisdom for the Christian Leader

Leadership inevitably brings moments when integrity feels costly. Pressure to conform, to protect momentum, or to avoid conflict can make it tempting to ignore what is wrong in order to preserve what is comfortable. Joshua 1:9 reminds leaders that courage is not the absence of fear but the resolve to move forward with conviction because God is present in the decision. When leaders rely only on approval or popularity for confidence, they become fragile. When they root their courage in God's presence, they can stand firm even when the path ahead creates tension.

Courageous leadership is not loud or reckless. It is steady, principled, and anchored in what is right. Leaders who bring truth into uncomfortable spaces protect the people they serve and strengthen the moral foundation of their organizations. The cost may show up in strained relationships or short-term resistance, but the impact runs deeper. Choosing integrity safeguards the mission and sets a tone that others will remember. When leaders step forward with courage, they create cultures where truth is valued, trust grows, and God's presence shapes the future.

Weekly Practice in Faith

This week, identify one situation where you know obedience requires courage. It might be a conversation you have been avoiding, a boundary you have been hesitant to set, or a decision you have delayed out of fear. Bring it before God in prayer. Ask Him to strengthen your resolve and give you clarity. Then take one step forward in faith, trusting that His presence will sustain you.

Time for Reflection

Consider where fear may be influencing your leadership more than you realize. Are there areas where you have chosen comfort over conviction? Have you delayed action because the personal or professional cost felt too high?

Joshua 1:9 is not simply encouragement. It is a command to lead with strength and courage because God goes with you. Ask God to reveal where you need greater boldness. Invite Him to replace fear with faith and hesitation with obedience.

Weekly Prayer

Father, give me courage to lead with obedience and faith. Help me stand firm in truth, even when it is costly. Amen.

WEEK 4

Two or More is a Strategy

"Two are better than one, because they have a good return for their labor: If either of them falls down, one can help the other up."

Ecclesiastes 4:9–12 (NIV)

We often fall into the mindset that leadership is a solo assignment. In reality, it is the opposite. No matter how skilled, experienced, or driven a leader may be, there are challenges that are simply too complex, too heavy, or too demanding to carry alone. God designed leadership to function within community, not only for encouragement but for partnership and shared strength.

Ecclesiastes 4 reminds us that "two are better than one." Not because it sounds cooperative, but because it works. Shared effort produces greater return. When one person stumbles, another can offer support. When one struggles to see clearly, another may provide perspective. When the path forward feels overwhelming, a team united in purpose and prayer can accomplish what no individual can accomplish alone.

Wise leaders recognize this. They resist isolation and instead lean into the gifts, insight, and problem-solving ability of those around them. This is not a weakness. It is wisdom. Whether in a business, ministry, classroom, or community setting, most significant breakthroughs are the result of collaborative effort. This week, consider how you approach leadership challenges. Do you carry them alone, or do you allow others to help share the weight?

Leadership Wisdom for the Christian Leader

Strong leaders recognize that individual talent will take an organization only so far. Ecclesiastes reminds us that two are better than one, and that principle speaks directly to modern leadership. Problems become lighter when shared, and blind spots shrink when others contribute their insight. Leaders who insist on carrying every burden alone often wear themselves thin and limit the impact of their teams. Collaboration is not a sign of weakness. It is a sign of wisdom. When leaders value the contributions of others, they create environments where solutions grow from collective effort rather than isolated struggle.

Working together also creates resilience. When one person falters, another can help them rise. This is the kind of support that strengthens teams and protects organizations during difficult seasons. Scripture shows that God works through community, and that shared labor produces a return no individual can create on their own. Leaders who embrace unity model humility, deepen trust, and build cultures that can withstand pressure. When you invite others into the work, you multiply not only productivity but also hope, strength, and endurance.

Weekly Practice in Faith

This week, identify one task, project, or responsibility where you tend to operate independently. Instead of handling it alone, intentionally invite others to contribute. Seek out people whose strengths and perspectives differ from yours. Listen to their ideas. Share ownership of the outcome.

Pay attention to what happens when you release control. Notice how trust grows, how creativity surfaces, and how the burden becomes lighter when it is carried together.

Time for Reflection

Ecclesiastes 4:9–12 highlights the strength that comes through partnership. Leadership was never meant to be a solitary path. Even the most capable leaders will grow weary at times, and God provides others to help carry what is too heavy alone.

Reflect on your current leadership environment. Do you tend to isolate when pressure increases, or do you invite others into the process? Are you willing to rely on the support God has given, or do you still feel the need to hold everything yourself? Ask God to reveal where pride, fear, or control may be keeping you from leading in true community.

Weekly Prayer

Lord, thank You for the people You have placed around me. Teach me to value teamwork and to serve alongside others with humility and joy. Amen.

WEEK 5

Making Decisions in Tough Times

"So, do not fear, for I am with you; do not be dismayed, for I am your God. I will strengthen you and help you; I will uphold you with my righteous right hand."

Isaiah 41:10 (NIV)

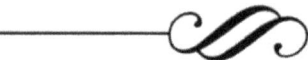

Every leader eventually faces moments where decisions feel heavy and uncertain. These are the seasons when the outcome is unclear, the pressure is high, and the responsibility feels isolating. In these moments, leadership is not just tested operationally. It is tested spiritually.

God does not promise a life without hardship, but He does promise His presence within it. Isaiah 41:10 reminds us that fear does not have to dominate difficult seasons. God promises strength, help, and steady support. Leadership in tough times is not about appearing unshaken. It is about choosing faith even when you feel unsteady.

Jesus modeled this in the garden of Gethsemane. He did not hide from the weight before Him. He prayed. He surrendered. He obeyed. His response was not driven by comfort or certainty, but by trust. As leaders, we are invited to respond the same way, to pause, to seek God's heart, and to trust His presence when clarity feels incomplete.

The late Billy Graham once said, "No matter who we are or what our situation is, it is better to face life's problems with Jesus than to face them alone." Leadership is no different. When decisions feel heavy, bring them to the Lord. Ask Him for wisdom to guide your steps (Psalm 119:133), strength to endure your trials, and peace for what you cannot control. Let Him meet you in the tension and carry what you were never meant to carry alone.

Hard decisions reveal where leadership is truly rooted, not in control, but in dependence, not in certainty, but in surrender. They expose what we trust most when outcomes are unclear and approval is uncertain. In those moments, leadership shifts from performance to discipleship, not just for you, but for those watching how you respond.

When you choose faith over fear, you teach your team how to handle pressure with spiritual maturity. When you slow down instead of rushing for control, you create space for God to move. Difficult decisions do not just shape results, they shape people. And when those decisions are surrendered to God, they become moments where He strengthens both your leadership and your faith.

Leadership Wisdom for the Christian Leader

Leaders make countless decisions, but the ones made under pressure leave the deepest imprint. In difficult seasons, fear often pushes leaders toward control, isolation, or rushed conclusions. But Scripture invites leaders to respond differently, not by denying fear, but by placing it into God's hands.

Isaiah 41:10 teaches leaders that strength is not drawn from self-reliance but from divine support. When leaders bring their uncertainty before God, they gain clarity that does not come from analysis alone. Decisions shaped by prayer, humility, and trust produce more than solutions. They produce stability.

Leadership grounded in God's presence builds confidence in those watching. Teams learn courage not from a leader's speech, but from a leader's posture. When a leader chooses faith instead of panic, others follow that example.

Hard decisions do more than resolve problems. They form the emotional and spiritual climate of a team. When people observe how a leader handles pressure, they learn what that leader truly trusts. If decisions flow from anxiety or self-protection, fear spreads. But when decisions are shaped by calm dependence on

God, stability spreads instead. In this way, difficult moments become formative leadership moments. They either magnify fear or cultivate faith in those being led.

Weekly Practice in Faith

This week, choose one decision that feels heavy or unresolved. Instead of trying to solve it immediately, sit with God first. Pray honestly. Write down what you're afraid of, what you're trying to protect, and what you need to surrender. Then ask for wisdom to see the decision not just as a problem, but as a place where God wants to strengthen your leadership.

Time for Reflection

Difficult decisions often reveal what we trust most. When pressure rises, do you instinctively tighten control, withdraw, or become reactive? Or do you slow down, breathe, and invite God into the process?

Isaiah 41:10 reminds us that God's presence is not circumstantial. He does not draw back when decisions become unclear. He draws closer.

Reflect on a recent leadership decision made under pressure.
- What drove your response: fear, control, or faith?
- How might your posture have shaped those around you?

Ask God to help you lead from trust instead of tension.

Weekly Prayer

Father, when the weight of leadership feels heavy, remind me that I am not carrying it alone. Teach me to lead from surrender instead of fear, from faith instead of control. Strengthen me to trust Your presence when decisions feel unclear. Let my posture bring stability to others as You bring stability to me. Amen.

A 52-Week Devotional for Leaders

Leadership and the Cross

COMMUNICATION

> **Weeks 6 - 10**
>
> Communication matters because it articulates vision, unifies teams around a shared purpose, builds trust, and aligns people on goals and expectations. For Christians, it is more than having a vision and a set of objectives. Rather, it is choosing a message, tone, and timing that align with Scripture and character. Over the next five weeks you will practice listening deeply, speaking with integrity and grace, addressing conflict with truth and humility, and encouraging others with clarity. The aim is Christ-centered communication that builds trust, brings healing, and advances the mission.

WEEK 6

The Power of Words

"The tongue has the power of life and death,
and those who love it will eat its fruit."

Proverbs 18:21 (NIV)

Words are never neutral. They can strengthen a discouraged heart or unravel trust in a moment. As a leader, your voice carries weight because people look to you for direction, clarity, and stability. Scripture reminds us that the tongue can produce life or destruction, and the difference often comes down to the intention behind what you say and how you say it.

Leadership communication goes deeper than delivering instructions. It reveals your inner posture. When your heart is aligned with Christ, your words become instruments of encouragement, clarity, and wisdom. When communication is hurried or careless, it can create confusion and unintended harm.

This week, take time to examine the spiritual posture behind your speech. Ask God to shape your heart so that your words become a steady source of strength for those you lead.

Leadership Wisdom for the Christian Leader

In leadership settings, words do more than convey information, they shape emotional and relational climate. A leader's tone can steady a team in difficult moments, while reactive or harsh language can undermine morale even when the message itself is necessary.

Healthy communication requires restraint, clarity, and empathy. Leaders rooted in Christ understand that truth and grace must work together. They avoid using words to assert control or express frustration, and instead speak in ways that invite responsibility, collaboration, and forward movement.

Life-giving communication does more than avoid harm. It creates space for honesty, trust, and growth. When leaders choose words that clarify rather than confuse, build rather than bruise, and guide rather than overwhelm, their teams respond with confidence and commitment.

Leaders should also pay attention to the timing of their words, not just their content. Even a true message can damage trust if it is delivered carelessly, publicly, or without discernment. Wisdom in communication often requires patience, waiting for the right moment, the right setting, and the right posture. When leaders learn to speak at the right time and not just with the right words, their communication becomes far more effective and far more honoring to God. It shows maturity, emotional discipline, and respect for both the truth and the people receiving it.

Weekly Practice in Faith

Choose one meaningful conversation you need to have this week. Before you speak, pause and pray: "Lord, shape my heart so my words reflect You." Then approach the conversation with intention, clarity, and grace. Pay attention not only to what you say, but to how you say it.

Time for Reflection

Words leave lasting impressions. Think back on a recent conversation where your tone, timing, or choice of words had a noticeable impact.
- What did it reveal about your heart in that moment?
- What might God be inviting you to refine in how you speak?

Ask the Holy Spirit to help you become a leader whose words consistently bring peace, clarity, and Christlike character into every space you enter.

Weekly Prayer

Lord, help me speak with wisdom and humility. Guard my words so that they bring clarity instead of confusion and hope instead of discouragement. Make my voice an instrument of grace that reflects Your heart in every setting. Amen.

WEEK 7

The Power of Listening

"Everyone should be quick to listen,

slow to speak and slow to become angry."

James 1:19 (NIV)

In a world full of noise, true listening has become rare. Many leaders feel pressure to respond quickly, defend positions, or move conversations forward. Yet godly leadership calls for something deeper. It calls for the discipline of listening, not just to spoken words, but to the hearts and needs behind them. Listening is not passive. It is an act of humility, patience, and spiritual attentiveness.

James 1:19 reminds us to be quick to listen, slow to speak, and slow to become angry. This posture reflects the heart of Christ. Jesus did not rush past people or dismiss their concerns. He paused for the blind, listened to the questions of His disciples, and responded to the quiet faith of those who reached for Him. His leadership was not shaped by urgency but by compassion and discernment.

As leaders, we are called to follow that example. Listening communicates respect, builds trust, and opens space for wisdom. It reminds people that their voice matters and that they are valued beyond their usefulness. It also reminds us that leadership is not about being heard first, but about understanding fully.

This week, slow your pace. Pay attention to conversations instead of rushing through them. Listen to those you lead, to God, and to what is happening beneath the surface of your environment.

Leadership Wisdom for the Christian Leader

James 1:19 gives leaders a posture that strengthens every team: quick to listen, slow to speak, slow to become angry. Many leaders feel pressure to respond fast, offer solutions, or fix morale with a pep talk. But wise leadership begins with listening.

When leaders pause long enough to hear what their people are actually experiencing, they gain insight that cannot be found in reports or performance metrics. Listening communicates humility and respect. It tells people their perspective matters, and that their leader values understanding more than control.

Being slow to speak creates space for honesty to surface, and being slow to anger helps leaders respond with clarity instead of reaction. Teams thrive when their leader builds trust through thoughtful presence rather than forceful direction. Listening does more than gather information. It restores connection, uncovers root problems, and reminds people they are seen. Leaders who embrace this posture create cultures where communication flows freely, issues are addressed early, and unity becomes possible again.

Weekly Practice in Faith

Think about a time when you needed someone to truly listen to you, a supervisor, a mentor, or a loved one, but felt unheard. How did that make you feel? Did it change your openness or trust?

This week, when someone comes to speak with you, make a deliberate choice to listen more than you talk. Put away distractions. Do not interrupt. Resist the urge to solve the problem immediately. Simply seek to understand fully. After the conversation, reflect on whether the other person felt heard and valued.

Time for Reflection

Listening is more than hearing words. It is valuing another person enough to give them your full attention. In leadership, it is easy to think we already know the issue or to rush toward solutions before understanding the root problem.

Consider a recent conversation where you focused more on your response than on truly hearing the other person. How might the outcome have changed if you had slowed down and listened with greater care? Ask God to help you develop a listening heart that reflects His patience, wisdom, and love toward others.

Weekly Prayer

Lord, teach me to listen with a quiet mind and a willing heart. Help me to hear not just words, but the needs, hopes, and concerns behind them. Shape me into a leader who values others by listening well and responding with wisdom and grace. Amen.

WEEK 8

Communicating with a Gentle Spirit

"Gracious words are a honeycomb,

sweet to the soul and healing to the bones."

Proverbs 16:24 (NIV)

Leadership is not just about what you say. It is about how your words are received. In a world that rewards being loud, fast, or clever, Scripture invites leaders into a different way: speaking with grace. Gracious words do more than transfer information. They heal tension, rebuild trust, and bring calm into moments of conflict.

Whether you are guiding a team, addressing a mistake, or offering correction, your tone matters. A gentle spirit does not make a leader weak. It reveals strength under control. It shows that your character governs your communication, not your emotions. Leaders who consistently choose grace over aggression are not only respected. They are remembered for making people feel seen, safe, and valued.

This week calls us to lead with both truth and tenderness. Gracious communication does not avoid hard conversations. It carries those conversations in a way that reflects the heart of Christ and leaves lasting impact instead of lasting wounds.

Leadership Wisdom for the Christian Leader

Every leader knows the tension that rises when pressure meets disappointment. It might be a missed deadline, a failed presentation, or a project that drifted off course. In those moments, tone becomes a turning point. One harsh sentence can deflate a team, shift a culture toward fear, and shut down honest communication. Yet a single gracious response can steady the room, calm anxious minds, and open a path toward real solutions. Leaders influence outcomes not only through decisions, but through the words they choose when emotions are high and eyes are watching.

Proverbs 16:24 teaches that gracious words bring sweetness and healing, and this truth cuts directly against the instinct many leaders feel in moments of tension. Pressure often tempts leaders to speak sharply or assert authority to regain control. But wise leadership understands that tone shapes culture, and that words spoken in frustration rarely produce growth.

Gracious communication does not avoid difficult truths. It delivers them in a way that preserves dignity and opens the door for honest conversation. When leaders choose grace over severity, they create conditions where people feel safe enough to take responsibility and engage in real problem solving.

Healing begins when words restore instead of wound. Teams are more willing to own mistakes, bring forward challenges, and offer solutions when they trust their leader's posture. Gracious words build that trust. They signal humility, maturity, and a commitment to the well being of the people doing the work. When a leader combines accountability with compassion, performance improves because people feel valued, not threatened. Leaders who speak life into difficult moments strengthen morale, deepen unity, and model the character of Christ in the way they guide those entrusted to them.

Weekly Practice in Faith

This week, intentionally invite the Holy Spirit into your conversations. Before engaging in a potentially difficult discussion, whether with a colleague, friend, or family member, pause and pray for a gentle spirit. Ask God to shape not only what you say, but how you say it.

As a practical step, slow your responses. Resist the urge to react quickly or defensively. Listen fully before speaking. Then ask yourself a simple question: Are the words I am about to speak shaped by grace or driven by frustration?

Time for Reflection

Words have the power to wound or to heal, to intensify conflict or to restore peace. As a leader, your communication sets the emotional tone for those around you. Gracious words do not weaken truth. They deliver it with care, restraint, and spiritual maturity.

Reflect on a recent moment when your words either calmed a situation or made it worse. What influenced the tone you chose? Was it patience, stress, fear, or faith? Ask God to refine your speech so that your words bring life, clarity, and restoration. Pray for wisdom to know when to speak, how to speak, and when silence may speak more powerfully than words.

Weekly Prayer

Lord, help me to speak with grace and listen with humility. Teach me to use my words to heal, not to harm; to build up, not to tear down. May my conversations reflect Your heart, filled with wisdom, mercy, and love. Shape my tone, my timing, and my truth so that every word I speak honors You. Amen.

WEEK 9

A Leader's Posture Speaks Volumes

"Let your light shine before others, that they may see your good deeds and glorify your Father in heaven."

Matthew 5:16 (NIV)

Leadership speaks long before you say a single word. The way you enter a room, sit at a table, or respond with a glance communicates something, whether you intend it or not. These nonverbal cues often carry more weight than spoken language. They can invite or intimidate, affirm or dismiss, open or shut down. A leader's posture reveals the posture of their heart.

Jesus modeled this perfectly. Long before He preached, He showed a leaders posture. He knelt to wash feet, touched the untouchable, and carried a cross for the sake of others. His posture was not only physical. It reflected His mission to serve. His presence communicated humility, compassion, and purpose long before His voice did.

As Christian leaders, how we carry ourselves matters. Presence, posture, and tone communicate just as clearly as words. This week, pay attention to the silent messages you send through your body language and demeanor. Your posture may be the first act of service someone experiences from you.

Leadership Wisdom for the Christian Leader

As a leader, have you ever walked into a room where the atmosphere felt heavy. Maybe people were guarded, conversations were clipped, or the tension was almost visible. In those moments, leaders have a choice. They can mirror the frustration in the room, or they can bring a different presence. A leader who enters with calm eyes, a steady spirit, and a posture of humility can shift the entire environment without saying a word. That subtle light, the kind that shows up through attitude and presence rather than authority, often becomes the spark that softens hearts and opens people to honest connection.

Matthew 5:16 reminds leaders that influence is not always expressed through big moments or grand gestures. Sometimes the clearest testimony comes through presence, posture, and the way a leader carries themselves in difficult seasons. Letting your light shine does not mean drawing attention to your talent or authority. It means reflecting the character of Christ in the way you show up. When leaders bring calm instead of tension, humility instead of defensiveness, and attentiveness instead of distraction, people notice. Light becomes visible through small decisions that signal care, respect, and intentionality.

This kind of leadership creates space for trust to grow. When team members feel seen and valued, they become more honest, more engaged, and more willing to repair what is broken. A leader's posture can soften hardened conversations and open doors that forcefulness would keep closed. Good deeds in leadership are often quiet acts of service: listening fully, being present, and creating environments where people can speak freely. When leaders let their light shine through steady, Christ centered character, the result points beyond them. It reveals a standard of grace, humility, and integrity that draws others upward and glorifies God in the everyday work of leadership.

Weekly Practice in Faith

This week, become more aware of how you communicate without speaking. During conversations, meetings, or casual interactions, pay attention to your posture, facial expressions, and eye contact. Are you open, calm, and present, or are you distracted, tense, or closed off?

Choose one recurring interaction with a coworker, friend, or family member. Practice being fully present. Put away your phone, relax your posture, and make intentional eye contact. Let your body language communicate attentiveness, respect, and a heart to serve rather than a need to control.

Time for Reflection

Leadership is not expressed only through decisions or direction. It is revealed through presence and demeanor. Jesus taught that His followers should let their light shine, not through showmanship, but through the way they live and serve.

Take time to examine the posture of your leadership. When you face pressure, success, or uncertainty, what do your actions communicate? Do they build trust? Do they reflect humility and service? Are you modeling a leadership presence that points others to Christ?

Ask God to shape not only what you say, but how you show up. Pray that your posture will reflect His grace, strength, and integrity in visible and invisible ways.

Weekly Prayer

Lord, help me serve not just with my hands, but with my presence. Teach me to lead with humility, to listen with compassion, and to reflect Your love in every unspoken way. May my posture point others to You. Amen.

WEEK 10

Speak with Integrity

"The Sovereign Lord has given me a well-instructed tongue,

to know the word that sustains the weary."

Isaiah 50:4 (NIV)

Words are not just tools for leaders. They are extensions of character. In leadership, communication is never neutral. It either builds trust or weakens it. When a leader speaks with integrity, their words carry weight because they reflect who they are and how they live, not just what they want others to hear.

Abraham Lincoln remains a strong historical example of this truth. During the Civil War, he did not lead only from a distance. He walked among the soldiers, listened to their fears, and spoke to their exhaustion and hope. His influence came not just from his position, but from his presence and consistency under pressure. People trusted his words because they matched his life. Leaders today build trust the same way when their communication is rooted in character and reinforced by their actions.

Scripture shows us this same alignment in the life of Jesus. He did not merely teach truth. He lived it. His words carried authority because His life supported them. He spoke with compassion to the broken, firmness to the proud, and clarity to those searching for direction. His communication was never driven by image or popularity, but by obedience and love.

Godly leaders are called to that same standard. Communication is not about eloquence or clever phrasing. It is about conviction, consistency, and Christlike care. Whether in a boardroom, classroom, ministry, or home, the way you speak reflects what you believe. Speak with truth. Speak with love. And speak from a life that practices what it proclaims.

Leadership Wisdom for the Christian Leader

In seasons of pressure or uncertainty, people watch their leaders more closely than they realize. It is often not the formal presentation or official announcement that stays with them, but the small moments of communication when a leader speaks with calm, presence, and clarity. One thoughtful conversation or one wise response can steady an entire team.

Isaiah 50:4 reminds us that God equips His leaders with words that sustain the weary. This calling goes beyond giving instructions or casting vision. It invites leaders to speak with spiritual responsibility and emotional awareness. People carry unseen burdens. Careless words can increase their weight, but words shaped by wisdom and humility can bring relief. When leaders communicate with sincerity and understanding, their words become a source of strength rather than pressure.

Sustaining the weary requires more than speaking well. It requires being present. Leaders who choose proximity over distance and conversation over avoidance earn trust because their words come from relationship, not position. They do not claim to have every answer. Instead, they offer steadiness, honesty, and reassurance. Through this kind of communication, leaders help their teams move through difficulty not by removing uncertainty, but by reminding them they are not alone.

Weekly Practice in Faith

This week, be intentional with how you communicate. Identify one situation where your instinct might be to avoid the conversation, delay it, or send a rushed response. Instead, choose presence.

Speak clearly, gently, and with care. Whether in person, by phone, or through a thoughtful message, let your tone reflect humility and sincerity.

Consider encouraging someone who seems worn down, addressing a misunderstanding you've ignored, or owning a mistake you have minimized. Remember, your words carry spiritual weight. Use them with purpose and prayer.

Time for Reflection

Words carry power, but integrity gives them lasting influence. As a leader, you are often called to speak into moments of uncertainty, tension, or discouragement. Isaiah 50:4 reminds us that our words should not only be wise, but Spirit-led and anchored in truth.

Reflect on your recent communication.
Are your words aligned with your character?
Do they bring clarity, peace, and encouragement, or do they create tension and confusion?

Ask God to shape your speech. Pray for discernment in your tone, patience in your responses, and compassion in your delivery. Let your words become instruments of His grace, not tools of control.

Weekly Prayer

Lord, help me lead not only with my words, but with integrity and presence. When it is easier to stay silent or withdraw, give me the courage to show up. Let my communication reflect Your truth, compassion, and faithfulness in every situation. Amen.

A 52-Week Devotional for Leaders

Leadership and the Cross

TRUST BUILDING

Weeks 11 - 15

Trust is the foundation of all effective leadership. But remember, it is not automatic. Trust must be cultivated through consistent, Christlike actions. Over the next five weeks, you' will explore how trust is built by leading with integrity, walking in humility, relying on God in uncertain times, guiding others through change with stability, and showing up with authentic presence. Trust is earned one choice at a time, and it always begins with how you lead yourself.

WEEK 11

Leading by Example Builds Trust

"Whatever you have learned or received or heard from me, or seen in me, put it into practice. And the God of peace will be with you."

Philippians 4:9 (NIV)

When we lead it is more than words or instruction. It is a lifestyle that others observe, follow, and often imitate. The apostle Paul understood this when he encouraged the Philippians not only to listen to his teachings but to model their lives after the way he lived out those teachings. He wasn't pointing to perfection. He was pointing to faith in action.

In today's workplace, ministry, or community, leaders are always being watched; whether they realize it or not. Teams notice how a leader handles conflict, responds to pressure, or treats others when no one is watching. The consistency between what a leader says and how they live is what builds real credibility. Leadership by example means embodying the values you want others to embrace. When others see a leader who leads with peace, conviction, and authenticity, it gives them permission to do the same. Paul's encouragement to "put it into practice" is not just a call to action. It is a call to alignment where belief and behavior walk hand in hand.

Leadership Wisdom for the Christian Leader

Some of the most influential lessons in leadership are not taught formally. They are absorbed through repetition, pattern, and atmosphere. The way a leader responds when plans fall apart. The patience they show when mistakes happen again. The discipline they maintain when no one is holding them accountable. These daily choices quietly define what a team believes leadership truly is. Over time, example becomes culture. And culture shapes everything from motivation to decision making.

Philippians 4:9 reminds leaders that influence is meant to be demonstrated, not just discussed. Paul challenges believers to practice what they have seen modeled before them. Leadership operates the same way. People do not separate belief from behavior. When a leader consistently models humility, responsibility, faithfulness, and patience, those values become visible standards for the entire team. What is practiced regularly becomes what is normalized.

This type of leadership cannot be manufactured. It grows slowly through daily integrity and quiet consistency. When leaders align their behavior with their convictions, trust begins to form without being forced. Teams become more unified, not through control, but through shared example. People follow more willingly when they trust the heart behind the actions. Leadership by example does not create perfection, but it does create stability, clarity, and a culture where people know what they are working toward.

Weekly Practice in Faith

This week, reflect on the example you're setting through your daily actions, both in public and in private settings. Identify one area where your leadership could better reflect Christlike character. Is it in how you respond under pressure? How you treat someone who challenges you? Or how you carry out responsibilities when no one is watching?

Time for Reflection

Leadership is revealed most clearly in the ordinary moments that few people applaud. The way you speak when frustrated, the choices you make when tired, and the consistency you show when no one is watching all communicate something about what you truly value. These quiet moments shape your influence more than visible accomplishments.

Take time to consider how your daily actions, habits, and decisions reflect your faith. Are your responses aligned with the example of Christ, especially under pressure or inconvenience? Think about one area where your leadership could grow stronger, whether in how you handle conflict, how you treat those who challenge you, or how you carry responsibility when no one is looking.

Instead of focusing only on how others view your leadership, pause and consider how God sees it. Are your private choices aligned with your public example? Ask God to bring clarity where alignment is needed and to strengthen your character so your life reflects His truth, whether you are observed or not.

Weekly Prayer

Lord, help me to lead in a way that honors You, not just with my words, but with my actions. Let my life reflect the integrity and love of Christ in every decision I make. May those around me see You through the way I serve, speak, and live. Amen.

WEEK 12

Being Humble Preserves Trust

"Humble yourselves before the Lord, and he will lift you up."

James 4:10 (NIV)

In leadership, humility is often misunderstood. Many see it as weakness or uncertainty. But in God's design, humility is the foundation of true strength. While the world celebrates status, visibility, and control, Jesus modeled something radically different. He chose service. He knelt. He lifted others. His humility was not passive. It was a deliberate posture of obedience and love.

James 4:10 reminds us that leadership is not built on self promotion but on surrender. When leaders humble themselves before God, they release the need to prove, defend, or dominate. They trust God to shape their influence and establish their impact. He does not elevate leaders through force or performance, but through faithfulness and obedience.

As Christian leaders, we are not called to climb. We are called to kneel. Humility places God at the center of our leadership and removes ego from the throne. When we lead from that posture, our influence becomes rooted in His power rather than our own image.

Leadership Wisdom for the Christian Leader

In the workplace, the loudest voice often gets the most attention. But the leaders who make the deepest impact are rarely the ones who dominate the room. They are the ones who ask thoughtful questions, elevate other voices, and approach responsibility with a steady posture rather than a spotlight. People remember leaders who invite them into the work, especially in seasons of uncertainty. Humility, when practiced consistently, becomes a quiet force that draws people together rather than pushing them away.

James 4:10 calls leaders to humble themselves before the Lord, trusting that God is the one who lifts up, establishes, and sustains. This runs counter to a culture that rewards self promotion and quick displays of authority. Humility in leadership is not weakness. It is strength under control. It frees leaders from the pressure to impress and allows them to focus on understanding, serving, and supporting those they lead. When a leader embraces humility, they create space for ideas to surface and for people to participate meaningfully in the work.

A humble leader builds trust because their actions are grounded in sincerity rather than ego. This posture strengthens collaboration, encourages open dialogue, and fosters unity during challenging seasons. As humility takes root, teams feel respected and valued, and they naturally respond with greater engagement and ownership. God lifts up leaders who choose this path, blessing their influence and shaping the culture around them. In the end, humility becomes more than a leadership style. It becomes a reflection of Christ at work within the leader and through the leader.

Weekly Practice in Faith

This week, practice humility through intentional restraint. Step back at least once to let someone else's voice lead the conversation. Invite another perspective before offering your own opinion.

Look for an opportunity to serve quietly without needing recognition. That may mean supporting a teammate behind the scenes, taking on an overlooked responsibility, or offering encouragement without seeking credit. Let your leadership be defined by service rather than visibility.

Time for Reflection

Humility does not reduce your leadership. It refines it. It positions your heart to receive God's direction instead of relying only on your own strength. In leadership, it can feel easier to project control than to surrender.

Ask yourself honestly: Are you giving God room to lead you?
Are you open to correction and guidance?
Do you seek input from others or resist it?

True humility does not make you smaller. It makes God larger in your leadership. Take time to surrender your posture, your plans, and your ambition to His will. Let Him shape not just what you do, but the spirit from which you lead.

Weekly Prayer

Lord, quiet my pride and help me lead with a heart that honors You. Remind me that true strength is found in surrender and that real influence comes from serving others. Teach me to trust Your timing and to walk humbly, knowing You will lift me up when the time is right. Amen.

WEEK 13

Having Accountability Fortifies Trust

"When you make a vow to God, do not delay to fulfill it.

He has no pleasure in fools; fulfill your vow."

Ecclesiastes 5:4 (NIV)

A leader is not measured by the promises they make, but by the commitments they keep. Vision and charisma may inspire people for a moment, but trust is built through consistency over time. When leaders follow through, they demonstrate respect, reliability, and integrity. When they do not, trust erodes, even if their intentions were good.

Scripture is clear about the weight of our words. Jesus said in Matthew 5:37, "All you need to say is simply 'Yes' or 'No.'" Our word should be enough. Luke 16:10 reinforces this by reminding us that faithfulness in small things reveals whether we can be trusted with greater responsibility. God is concerned not only with our big promises, but with our daily reliability.

Accountability in leadership is not about never failing. It is about owning what you said, acknowledging when you fall short, and doing what is required to make it right. Leaders who take responsibility, especially when it is uncomfortable, build credibility that speeches and vision alone cannot create. Over time, that credibility becomes the foundation upon which lasting trust is built.

Leadership Wisdom for the Christian Leader

Whether among a team or an entire organization, people learn quickly whether a leader's words carry weight. A commitment can energize a team, but an unkept promise can drain trust faster than any mistake. Leaders often underestimate how closely teams watch for follow through. A simple pledge to improve processes, communicate better, or provide support creates an expectation that shapes morale. When action does not match intention, people do not become cynical overnight. They become disappointed. Over time, they stop believing the words that once motivated them.

Ecclesiastes 5:4 gives leaders a sobering reminder. When you make a vow, fulfill it. God takes integrity seriously, because integrity shapes influence. In leadership, promises are not just expressions of hope. They are commitments that build credibility. Good intentions are never enough. Follow through is what demonstrates character. When leaders delay, minimize, or abandon what they pledged to do, they weaken the trust that healthy teams depend on. But when they act with consistency, even small steps rebuild confidence and honor God.

Integrity grows as leaders align their words with their actions. This does not require perfection. It requires accountability. Leaders who revisit their commitments, communicate progress, and invite feedback show their teams that promises matter. Such leaders create cultures where reliability is valued, expectations are clear, and people feel secure. God lifts up leaders who take their vows seriously, not because they are flawless, but because they are faithful. Their steady commitment becomes a testimony that leadership is not measured by speeches, but by the integrity that follows them.

Weekly Practice in Faith

This week, identify one responsibility, large or small, that you have delayed, forgotten, or avoided. Acknowledge it honestly. Do not excuse it. Then take one clear, practical step toward following through.

If someone else has been affected, communicate with them directly. Take ownership. Explain your next steps. Accountability is not about shame. It is about restoring trust through action. Let this become a rhythm, not a one time correction.

Time for Reflection

Think about a time when you gave your word but struggled to follow through. What got in the way? Was it fear, distraction, overcommitment, or pride?

Ecclesiastes 5:4 reminds us that God does not take our commitments lightly. What we promise, especially in His name or in His presence, carries weight. Reflect on your leadership today. Are there commitments you have delayed or abandoned? Are there areas of obedience God has been prompting you to complete?

Ask Him for clarity and courage. Reflection is not meant to produce guilt. It is meant to awaken responsibility. Take one step today toward alignment between what you say and what you do.

Weekly Prayer

Lord, help me to be faithful in the small things. Make my words match my actions and give me the humility to own my missteps. Teach me to lead with integrity, follow through with care, and build trust with those around me. I want my leadership to reflect Your character; faithful, true, and consistent. Amen.

WEEK 14

Create a Safe Place For Your Team

"Accept one another,

then, just as Christ accepted you"

Romans 15:7 (NIV)

Every leader wants to see their team thrive, contribute fully, and give their best to the mission. But that does not happen in cultures driven only by performance metrics or polished speeches. Flourishing begins with trust, and trust begins with safety.

Psychological safety is the confidence people feel when they can speak honestly, ask questions, make mistakes, and share ideas without fear of embarrassment or rejection. It does not remove accountability. It creates an environment where accountability can exist without humiliation.

As leaders who honor Christ, we are called to reflect the welcoming heart of Jesus. Romans 15:7 says, "Accept one another, then, just as Christ accepted you, in order to bring praise to God."

When our posture is marked by acceptance rather than judgment, people feel permission to show up fully rather than hide their voice. Over time, safety creates courage. It invites honesty, creativity, and growth. The goal is not comfort at any cost, but Christlike care that strengthens truth and transformation.

Leadership Wisdom for the Christian Leader

Sometimes the clearest sign that a team is struggling is not a missed deadline or a drop in performance. It is the silence that exists within the team meeting. Ideas stop flowing. People hold back from asking questions. The atmosphere feels cautious all because there is a fear or concern they will be negative consequences. This fear of retribution is identified as a lack of psychological safety. When this occurs, even the strongest talent will eventually withdraw. Leaders often look for strategic fixes, but the real issue is relational. People flourish where they feel accepted, respected, and free to speak without fear.

Romans 15:7 calls leaders to accept others just as Christ accepted them, fully and without hesitation. This challenges leaders to go beyond politeness or surface level affirmation. Acceptance in leadership means creating an environment where people feel safe to express ideas, raise concerns, and show up as themselves. It means listening without judgment and valuing each person's contribution. When leaders cultivate acceptance, they open the door for honesty, innovation, and trust. Psychological safety is not a modern trend. In fact, Jesus recognized practiced psychological safety through his teachings and actions. We can see this in the way he invited people come to him and deliver their burdens. In return, Jesus accepted them and promised to listen, all while they felt safe in his presence.

Psychological safety shapes the culture of a team. Leaders who respond with curiosity instead of defensiveness build trust that cannot be manufactured any other way. When criticism is met with humility and diverse voices are encouraged, people begin to reengage. They bring forward ideas that had been quiet. They address problems early instead of carrying them silently.

A culture of psychological safety strengthens commitment because people feel seen and valued and they are not afraid to speak up. Leaders who practice this kind of Christlike acceptance create workplaces where people are free to grow, contribute, and thrive.

Weekly Practice in Faith

This week, intentionally create space for others to feel safe, valued, and heard. Identify one environment or relationship where people seem hesitant to speak freely. It may be your workplace, your ministry setting, or your own home.

Take one deliberate step to shift the atmosphere. Invite honest feedback. Ask open ended questions. Resist interrupting or defending. Simply listen. Psychological safety often grows through small, consistent choices. Over time, your steady posture of humility and openness will shape a culture where people feel secure enough to speak truth.

Time for Reflection

Romans 15:7 calls us to accept others just as Christ accepted us. Reflect on how this principle shows up in your leadership. Do people feel safe to speak openly around you? Are they comfortable sharing ideas, concerns, or even disagreements?

This is not just about tolerance. It is about creating an environment where people experience genuine acceptance. Consider your current leadership context. Whose voice is being overlooked? Who may feel unheard or hesitant? Ask God how your leadership posture can better reflect the open arms of Christ this week.

Weekly Prayer

Lord, thank You for accepting me fully and without condition. Help me lead others with that same spirit of grace and openness. Teach me to listen with empathy, to speak with care, and to create safe spaces where people feel seen, heard, and valued.

Where there is fear, let me bring calm. Where there is silence, let me invite voice. And where there is hurt, let me offer healing through humility and love. I pray that my leadership would reflect the welcome of Christ and build a culture where trust can grow. Amen.

WEEK 15

Authenticity Fosters Trust

"Dear children, let us not love with words or speech

but with actions and in truth."

1 John 3:18 (NIV)

Authentic leadership is not about saying the right things or managing a polished image. It is about leading from a place of truth, integrity, and alignment with your values. In a world that often rewards appearance over substance, authentic leaders stand out because they are consistent. They are the same in public and in private, in high pressure spaces and quiet moments. That consistency builds trust and invites others into deeper respect and connection.

Authenticity means walking in the light even when it is uncomfortable or costly. First John 3:18 reminds us that love, and by extension leadership, is proven through action, not just speech.

Words without truth behind them fade quickly, but actions rooted in commitment and conviction endure. When your leadership reflects both who you are and whose you are, it becomes a living testimony.

When leaders drop the mask and lead from truth, credibility follows. They also create space for others to do the same. This week is an invitation to lead with your whole self, grounded in faith, guided by conviction, and free from pretense.

Leadership Wisdom for the Christian Leader

There are seasons when a leader's words begin to fall flat, not because the audience is resistant, but because authenticity is no longer sensed. When leaders lose concern for the past that shaped their organization, the present that sustains it, or the future they are responsible to steward, people feel it. What remains are symptoms; dishonesty instead of transparency, a lack of empathy for those carrying the work, poor communication that creates confusion, and decisions driven more by personal comfort than collective well being. In those moments, people are not asking for better speeches or stronger messaging. They are longing for leaders who care enough to be honest, present enough to listen, and grounded enough to lead with integrity rather than self interest.

First John 3:18 reminds leaders that truth is proven through action, not talk. When words have lost their weight, only consistent behavior can restore what has been damaged. Authentic leadership is not built on charisma, image, or polished delivery. It is built on honesty, humility, and consistency over time. Leaders begin to rebuild trust when they acknowledge where they have failed, speak clearly about what is real, and align their decisions with the values they claim to hold, even when it costs them.

Authenticity does not make a leader flawless, but it makes them credible. And credible leadership has power. When people see a leader who is willing to own mistakes, listen with sincerity, and follow through with integrity, space is created for trust to return. Over time, this consistency breaks down fear, encourages openness, and invites people to engage again.

When leaders live their values instead of merely talking about them, teams feel it. They lower their guard. They step forward. They trust. That alignment between who a leader claims to be and how they actually lead reflects the character of Christ and cultivates an environment where truth, trust, and growth can finally take root.

Weekly Practice in Faith

This week, take one deliberate step toward authenticity. Share something truthful with someone you lead or serve alongside. It could be a lesson you have learned, an area where you're still growing, or a moment where you stumbled and had to course correct.

Do not share simply to be vulnerable. Share to build trust. Let your honesty create space for others to show up more fully and truthfully as well.

Time for Reflection

Authenticity is not about perfection. It is about alignment between your words, actions, and values. When those areas are consistent, people experience your leadership as sincere and trustworthy.

Reflect on your leadership posture right now. Are there places where you say one thing but live another? Are some decisions driven more by approval than conviction? Are you leading from truth or managing perception?

Take time to bring those questions before God. Ask Him to reveal any misalignment. Invite Him to strengthen your courage to lead with consistency, transparency, and integrity so that others experience leadership shaped by truth and love.

Weekly Prayer

Lord, help me lead with honesty and integrity. In moments when I'm tempted to perform or pretend, remind me that You have called me to be real, not perfect. Shape my character to reflect Your truth, so that my leadership earns trust and gives glory to You. Amen.

Leadership and the Cross

THE LEADER'S CALLING

Weeks 16 - 20

Leadership is not just about talent or title, but about answering a deeper call; one that reflects the character of Christ in how we serve, respond, and lead. Over the next five weeks, you'll explore five expressions of that calling. You'll learn from the Servant Leader who lifts others above self, the Spirit-Filled Leader who stays in step with God's guidance, the Leader of Change who navigates transition with wisdom, the Transformational Leader who inspires growth, and the Situational Leader who adapts to meet real needs. Together, these models remind us that godly leadership begins with surrender, thrives through faithfulness, and leaves a lasting impact.

WEEK 16

The Call to be a Servant Leader

"Just as the Son of Man did not come to be served, but to serve, and to give his life as a ransom for many."

Matthew 20:28 (NIV)

Today's culture often equates leadership with authority, influence, and status. Titles are celebrated and power is pursued. But Jesus completely overturned that model. In Matthew 20:28, He made it clear that greatness in the Kingdom of God is not measured by how many people serve you, but by how well you serve others. The Son of God, who had every right to demand allegiance, instead chose humility. He washed feet, touched the rejected, and gave His life for people who did not yet understand who He truly was.

Servant leadership is not weak or passive. It is a deliberate decision to put others first, not because they deserve it, but because it mirrors the heart of Christ. Servant leaders do not lead to elevate themselves. They lead to lift others. They focus less on control and more on compassion. Less on being right and more on being righteous. They give away credit. They accept responsibility. They notice the needs that others ignore.

Jesus demonstrated this clearly in John 13:3–16 when He knelt to wash His disciples' feet. He placed Himself in the role of a servant, removing the dust and dirt from the feet of the very men who would later abandon Him. In doing so, He taught them what Christlike leadership truly looks like. He was not just performing an act of humility. He was redefining greatness. When He told them, "Unless I wash you, you have no part with me," He was showing that true leadership flows from love, humility, and service.

In a world that teaches us to climb higher, Jesus invites us to kneel lower. His leadership was rooted in love, humility, and obedience, and it transformed everything. When we lead like Him, we stop chasing recognition and start pursuing redemption in our teams, our families, our organizations, and within our own hearts.

Leadership Wisdom for the Christian Leader

In our workplaces, people can sense right away whether a leader is there to gain something or to give something. You see it in how they show up, how they listen, and how they engage with the people doing the everyday work. Some leaders enter a room expecting to be served. Others step in ready to serve. That difference, though subtle at first, becomes the defining factor in whether a team feels valued or merely used.

Matthew 20:28 offers a clear and countercultural model for leadership. Jesus describes His mission not in terms of authority or status, but in terms of service. Leaders who follow His example recognize that influence is not a tool for personal advancement. It is an opportunity to elevate others. Serving as a leader does not mean avoiding responsibility or shying away from difficult decisions. It means approaching those responsibilities with humility, empathy, and a willingness to shoulder burdens rather than shift them downward. When leaders lead with a servant's heart, people feel seen rather than managed.

Servant leadership builds trust because it demonstrates sincerity. Teams respond differently when they know their leader is willing to step into hard moments with them. Service creates belonging. It strengthens collaboration. It cultivates loyalty. When leaders choose to serve first and lead second, the atmosphere shifts from hierarchy to shared purpose. This posture reflects the heart of Christ and becomes a powerful witness in the workplace. True leadership is not measured by how many people follow, but by how well a leader serves the ones entrusted to them.

Weekly Practice in Faith

This week, identify one specific opportunity to serve someone within your circle of influence at work, at home, or in your community. Choose an act of service that meets a real need but may not receive recognition. Offer to help lighten a coworker's workload. Support a family member who is overwhelmed. Give your undivided attention to someone who feels overlooked.

As you serve, remind yourself that this is not about earning appreciation, but about reflecting Christ. Serve with humility. Serve with quiet faithfulness. Let your actions be an expression of obedience, not applause.

Time for Reflection

Jesus redefined leadership by placing service above status. His example shows that the greatest influence often comes through humble, unseen acts of love. Leadership rooted in service is not focused on personal gain. It is focused on lifting others, meeting needs, and reflecting God's character.

Reflect on your leadership this week. Are your decisions shaped more by self interest or by a sincere desire to support and strengthen others? Do you serve only when it is visible, or are you willing to serve when no one notices?

Ask God to form in you the heart of a servant. Pray that your leadership will move from self promotion to self donation, becoming a reflection of Christ's sacrificial love.

Weekly Prayer

Lord, You came not to be served, but to serve. Help me reflect that same posture in my leadership. Remove any pride or entitlement that keeps me from doing the small, unseen acts of service. Teach me to lead with compassion, to value people over position, and to recognize the sacredness in every task. May others see You through the way I serve them this week. Amen.

WEEK 17

The Call to be a Spirit-Filled Leader

"Since we live by the Spirit, let us keep in step with the Spirit."

Galatians 5:25 (NIV)

Leadership is not simply about charisma, credentials, or communication skill. At its core, leadership is about influence; how we guide, shape, and serve others. But what distinguishes Christian leadership from all other forms is the source of that influence: the Holy Spirit. Spirit-filled leadership does not begin in the boardroom or the pulpit. It begins in the quiet, surrendered heart of a leader who walks daily with God.

To be led by the Spirit is to lead with divine wisdom rather than human instinct. It means responding rather than reacting, discerning rather than demanding, and trusting rather than controlling. Leaders who live this way operate from a different source of strength. Their presence carries peace, their words carry clarity, and their decisions carry weight because they are being led even as they lead.

Spirit-filled leadership also gives people more than instructions. It gives them meaning. God never intended His people to simply perform tasks without purpose. When Moses led the Israelites out of Egypt, he did more than direct their movement through the wilderness. He consistently reminded them they were God's chosen people, headed toward a promised land. Their hardship was not random. Their journey had purpose. He gave meaning to their obedience and identity to their struggle.

In the same way, Spirit-filled leaders today must help people see the "why" behind what they do. People do not disengage because work is hard. They disengage because it feels empty. But when leaders connect daily responsibilities to a larger purpose, rooted in God's calling, something shifts. Work becomes service. Tasks become stewardship. Effort becomes worship. This kind of leadership creates belonging, not just productivity.

Galatians 5:25 reminds us that the Spirit is not just a theological idea, but a practical guide: "Since we live by the Spirit, let us keep in step with the Spirit." This means slowing down to listen, submitting decisions to prayer, and aligning leadership choices with God's direction rather than personal ambition. A Spirit-filled leader does not only direct people. He or she shepherds hearts, purposes, and meaning.

Leadership Wisdom for the Christian Leader

Organizations often focus on productivity, deadlines, and numbers, while quietly neglecting the human and spiritual needs of their people. When purpose fades and connection weakens, motivation declines, engagement drops, and burnout rises. People stop seeing meaning in what they do and begin to feel invisible in the process. In those moments, what they need most is not pressure, but leadership that reconnects them to purpose and belonging.

Spirit-led leadership addresses more than performance. It speaks to the heart. By keeping in step with the Spirit, leaders bring clarity of vision to confused environments, restore hope where discouragement has taken root, and demonstrate genuine care that builds belonging. This is not emotional leadership. It is spiritual leadership shaped by God's presence.

When leaders operate from faith rather than fear, they create stability. When they lead from love rather than control, they build trust. When they communicate vision rather than only demands, they give people something meaningful to move toward. A Spirit-filled leader does more than manage behavior. They cultivate purpose, strengthen relationships, and foster a culture where people feel called, valued, and connected.

Such leadership does not eliminate pressure, but it redemptively reframes it. It reminds people they are not driven only by deadlines, but held within a larger purpose. It builds a sense of shared mission where individuals are not just employees, but contributors to something God is doing. That is when leadership moves from task management to spiritual influence.

Weekly Practice in Faith

This week, take a step toward Spirit-filled leadership by focusing on purpose and people, not just performance.

First, identify one place in your leadership where people may lack clarity or connection. Ask yourself: Do they know why their work matters? Do they feel seen and valued?

Choose one intentional action:

- Clearly restate the purpose behind a task or project.

- Speak hope into a discouraged person or team.

- Express appreciation for someone who feels unseen.

Before acting, take time in prayer and ask the Holy Spirit to guide your words and posture. Let your leadership reflect God's vision, God's love, and God's faithfulness through small but intentional steps.

Time for Reflection

Spirit-filled leadership does not begin with action; it begins with alignment. When you lead from the Spirit, you offer more than direction. You offer meaning, belonging, and hope.

Reflect on your leadership today.
Are you helping people see purpose or only pressure?
Are you fostering belonging or merely managing tasks?
Are you operating from fear or from faith?

Ask God to deepen your awareness of His Spirit at work in your leadership. Pray that your influence would not just accomplish tasks, but draw people toward His vision, His love, and His truth.

Weekly Prayer

Lord, I surrender my leadership to You. Fill me with Your Spirit so that my decisions, actions, and words reflect Your wisdom and love. Help me to lead not by my own strength, but through Your guidance and power. In all I do, may others see not just my leadership, but Your presence within me. Amen.

WEEK 18

The Call to be a Leader of Change

"There is a time for everything,

and a season for every activity under the heavens."

Ecclesiastes 3:1 (NIV)

Change is inevitable, but how we lead through it defines our influence. Whether launching a new initiative, navigating uncertainty, or helping others embrace a new direction, leaders must learn to move with clarity, courage, and compassion. Scripture reminds us that change is not random disruption. Often, it is God's way of stretching our faith, refining our leadership, and preparing us for a greater purpose. Even when the reason behind a shift is unclear, it may be carrying divine intention.

As leaders, it is natural to resist change in favor of comfort or familiarity. We cling to old systems, strategies, or roles because they feel secure. Yet godly leadership requires the faith to follow God even when the path ahead is unfamiliar. That might mean releasing something that once worked. It might mean stepping into a new season of growth. It often means trusting that God is working behind the scenes even when we cannot see it. Ecclesiastes 3:1 reminds us that the seasons of leadership, beginnings, endings, and transitions, are not accidents. They are appointed.

This week, consider what changes you are facing. Are you clinging to what was, or are you seeking God's purpose in what is becoming? Change can be uncomfortable, but it can also be transformational. When leaders move forward with discernment and surrender, they reflect a leadership that trusts God's timing and aligns with His plan.

Leadership Wisdom for the Christian Leader

Leadership rarely unfolds within a stable or predictable rhythm. One season, a strategy works perfectly. The next, it falls flat. People change. Systems evolve. Organizations shift. Leaders often find themselves standing between what once worked and what now needs to be rebuilt. These moments create tension between holding on and letting go. How a leader responds in those moments shapes not just the outcome, but the culture and character of the leader themselves.

Ecclesiastes 3:1 reminds us that there is a time for everything and a season for every activity under heaven. For leaders, this means recognizing that God often works through transition rather than comfort or stability. Seasons of change are not signs of failure. They are invitations to discernment. When leaders cling tightly to the past, fear grows. When they approach change with prayer, humility, and openness, they begin to recognize God's hand guiding the process. Faith in leadership means releasing what was and trusting what God is forming next.

Healthy leadership sees purpose in every season. Some seasons refine skill. Others deepen character. Some stretch the team. Others stabilize it. When leaders surrender their need for control and allow God to shape their posture, they build resilience in themselves and in those they lead. Change becomes less of a threat and more of a tool in God's hands. Leaders who lead through seasons with trust and obedience cultivate cultures that adapt, grow, and ultimately flourish under God's timing and wisdom.

Weekly Practice in Faith

This week, identify one area in your leadership where change feels uncertain or uncomfortable. Instead of asking God to remove the situation, ask Him to transform you through it. Ask what He may be teaching you in the tension, whether patience, humility, trust, or courage. Allow your prayer to move from "make this easier" to "shape me through this."

Time for Reflection

As a leader, it can be tempting to cling to what is familiar, what once worked, what feels safe, or what others expect from you. But leadership requires the discernment to recognize when a new season has arrived and the courage to respond accordingly. God's design includes seasons of growth, pruning, rest, and renewal.

Take time to reflect on the season you are currently in. Are you trying to force something to continue that God may be inviting you to release? Are you resisting the new because it feels uncomfortable or unclear? Ask God for wisdom to lead with awareness of the season and for the faith to move forward even as the path changes.

Weekly Prayer

Lord, You are the God of all seasons; the One who brings new beginnings, endings, and everything in between. When change unsettles me, help me remember that You are already at work in the unknown. Shape me into a leader who embraces transformation, not with fear, but with faith. In every shift, remind me that You are constant. Amen.

WEEK 19

The Call to be a Transformational Leader

"Therefore, if anyone is in Christ, the new creation has come: The old has gone, the new is here!"

2 Corinthians 5:17 (NIV)

In a world shaped by rapid change, uncertainty, and increasing complexity, transformational leaders are needed more than ever. Not leaders who simply preserve what exists, but leaders who ignite lasting change from the inside out. History gives us examples such as Martin Luther King, Jr., Nelson Mandela, and Susan B. Anthony. Yet at the heart of all true transformation stands Jesus Christ. He did not simply improve what already existed. He reshaped reality itself. His life and message sparked radical change in individuals, communities, and entire cultures. He turned fishermen into apostles, outcasts into witnesses, and persecutors into preachers. His leadership was not superficial or transactional. It was soul deep, life shaping, and eternal.

Jesus did not only teach new ideas. He lived a new way of being. He did not demand change from a distance. He walked with people through it. He restored identity, reframed purpose, and called people into a future they never imagined for themselves. His invitation was simple: "Come, follow me." And when people did, everything changed. His leadership continues to transform hearts today because it is rooted in truth, grace, and redemption.

As Christian leaders, we are called to carry that same spirit of transformation. It starts with us. Before we can lead renewal in others, we must allow Christ to reshape our own hearts, thinking, and leadership posture. This means letting go of old habits, unlearning unhealthy patterns, and embracing the new life being formed in us through Him.

This week, reflect on how transformation is unfolding in your leadership. Are you simply managing processes, or are you influencing hearts? Are you repeating old patterns, or allowing Christ to renew your thinking? Transformation is not a single moment. It is a lifelong process of becoming more like Him for His glory and for the good of those you lead.

Leadership Wisdom for the Christian Leader

There are seasons when a team appears productive on the surface but feels empty underneath. Tasks get completed, results look fine, yet morale feels low and purpose feels thin. In those moments, wise leaders recognize that the issue is not operational. It is spiritual and cultural. A policy change or motivational speech will not solve it. What is needed is transformation at the heart level.

Second Corinthians 5:17 reminds us that in Christ, the old is gone and the new has come. This truth applies not only to salvation, but to leadership formation. When leaders allow God to renew their mindset, they begin to see their people differently. They prioritize development over output, purpose over pressure, and integrity over efficiency. A transformed leader becomes the catalyst for a transformed culture. Renewal begins in the leader before it takes root in the organization.

Transformation in leadership often starts with quiet, intentional shifts. Choosing to listen instead of react. Asking questions instead of issuing commands. Aligning motives with Kingdom values instead of performance metrics. When a leader models growth, humility, and authenticity, people notice. Hope begins to return. Trust begins to rebuild. The old ways start to fade, replaced with renewed energy and shared purpose. This is the power of Christ-centered leadership. When a leader becomes a new creation, the culture is invited to become one as well.

Weekly Practice in Faith

This week, take one intentional step toward developing transformation in others, not just performance. Identify one person you lead or influence who could benefit from encouragement or direction. Instead of fixing their problem, help them discover their potential. Ask questions that draw out their gifts. Speak life into their purpose. Model the character and growth you hope to see multiplied.

Time for Reflection

Leading others through change often mirrors God's renewing work in us. Old habits, outdated mindsets, and rigid leadership patterns can limit what God wants to do. Transformation begins when leaders surrender not only control, but comfort.

Reflect on the culture you help shape. Are you leading from patterns rooted in fear or self-preservation, or from a renewed heart anchored in Christ's vision? Ask God to replace quick fixes with lasting transformation, and to make your leadership an instrument of renewal where people, purpose, and culture are continually made new.

Weekly Prayer

Lord, renew my mind and reshape my heart. Help me resist the urge to conform to what the world expects and instead lead with vision, purpose, and truth. Transform me from the inside out so that my leadership reflects Your will and brings lasting impact to those I serve. Amen.

WEEK 20

The Call to be Situational Leader

"The prudent see danger and take refuge,

but the simple keep going and pay the penalty"

Proverbs 27:12 (NIV)

The Bible may not use the term "situational leadership," but its wisdom consistently highlights the importance of discernment, attentiveness, and wise timing. Proverbs 27:12 reminds us that prudent leaders do not rush forward blindly. They pay attention to shifting circumstances, anticipate what lies ahead, and respond with foresight instead of fear. This kind of leadership is steady, clear, and grounded, adjusting posture and approach with both wisdom and purpose.

Leadership is never static. What works in one season may fail in another, and the ability to read a situation often determines whether influence becomes fruitful or harmful. This is the heart of situational leadership: responding to people and circumstances with flexibility, without compromising conviction.

Scripture gives us clear examples of this. Jesus spoke firmly to the Pharisees, but tenderly to tax collectors and sinners. He comforted those who grieved, challenged those who were hardened, and taught in ways that met each audience where they stood. Nehemiah not only rebuilt walls; he discerned threats, motivated discouraged workers, and adjusted his strategy in the face of opposition. Esther demonstrated situational wisdom by understanding that timing and positioning were as critical as courage when she approached the king.

Situational leadership does not abandon principles. It applies them wisely. God-honoring leadership holds firm to truth while remaining sensitive to context. As you reflect this week, consider where God may be inviting you to slow down, listen more closely, or adjust your approach. The most effective leaders are not rigid, but discerning, able to recognize what others miss and respond with clarity, courage, and compassion.

Leadership Wisdom for the Christian Leader

Some leaders move through their week relying on routine, applying the same approach to every situation. Others practice situational awareness, recognizing that leadership must adjust as people and circumstances change. They notice what most overlook; a shift in tone, rising tension between colleagues, a team quietly struggling under new expectations, or the environment has evolved. These subtle cues rarely show up in data dashboards, yet they reveal the real state of the team. Leaders who pay attention are able to respond with the right action at the right time.

Proverbs 27:12 reminds us that the prudent see danger and take refuge, while the simple keep going and pay the penalty. Situational leadership embodies that wisdom. It means refusing to assume yesterday's strategy fits today's challenge. It means pausing long enough to evaluate what the moment calls for; more support, clearer direction, stronger accountability, or simply space to breathe. Wise leaders adjust their approach not out of inconsistency, but out of care for the people they lead.

Discernment is at the core of effective leadership. When leaders stay attentive and flexible, they protect the well-being of both the team and the mission. Small shifts in style, tone, or pace can prevent burnout, restore clarity, and strengthen trust. This kind of responsiveness mirrors the leadership of Christ, who met each person differently; offering healing to some, correction to others, and compassion to all. Situational leadership is not about being reactive, but being perceptive; choosing the response that best serves the moment and the people within it.

Weekly Practice in Faith

This week, pause and take inventory of a current leadership situation you are facing; whether at work, in volunteer service, or in your home. Ask yourself, "What is truly needed right now?" Is it guidance, encouragement, correction, or simply a listening ear?

Each day, commit to practicing spiritual situational awareness. Begin by praying for discernment and asking God to help you see beyond surface-level issues. Then challenge yourself to adjust your response not out of fear or convenience, but out of love and a desire to serve others faithfully.

Time for Reflection

Situational leadership is not about having all the answers. It is about paying close attention to what is unfolding around you. God calls leaders to be alert, aware, and discerning, recognizing when to move forward, when to pause, and when to seek refuge. This requires wisdom, not just boldness.

Take time to reflect on a current leadership situation in your life. Are you navigating it with prayerful discernment, or relying on assumptions? Are you paying attention to signs of burnout, tension, or shifting dynamics within those you lead?

Ask God to sharpen your awareness and give you courage to act wisely in the moment. Wise leaders adapt not out of anxiety, but out of faith in the One who sees the whole picture.

Weekly Prayer

Lord, help me to lead with eyes wide open and a heart tuned to Your Spirit. In every situation, give me the wisdom to pause, perceive, and respond with discernment. Teach me to let go of my desire for control and instead trust You to guide my leadership moment by moment. May my decisions reflect grace, truth, and care for those You've entrusted to me. Amen.

A 52-Week Devotional for Leaders

Leadership and the Cross

ORGANIZATIONAL CHANGE

Weeks 21 - 25

Change is inevitable, but how we lead through it reveals our character, faith, and readiness. Whether change is planned or unexpected, leaders are called to navigate uncertainty with courage and wisdom. Over the next five weeks, you'll reflect on why change happens, how to prepare for it, what to do when it's hard, how to stay steady through the process, and how to respond when it doesn't go as planned. With Scripture as your guide, you'll explore how godly leaders lead not just through outcomes, but through transformation.

WEEK 21

Understanding Why Change Occurs

"See, I am doing a new thing!
Now it springs up; do you not perceive it? I am making a way in the wilderness and streams in the wasteland."

Isaiah 43:19 (NIV)

The world we live in is bound by time and marked by constant change. Ecclesiastes 3:1 reminds us that for everything there is a season and a time for every purpose. Change is one of the few guarantees in life and in leadership. Yet when it arrives, especially when unexpected or unwanted, it can feel disruptive, inconvenient, or even threatening. It unsettles routines, challenges identities, and forces leaders to confront uncertainty. Resistance to change often stems less from pride and more from apprehension, specifically the fear of losing control, failing, or stepping into the unknown. Yet Scripture shows us that God is not only present in seasons of change. He frequently initiates them.

Isaiah 43:19 reminds us that God is always at work, even when we cannot yet see the full picture. "See, I am doing a new thing," He declares. But the deeper question remains: Do you perceive it? Can you recognize God's hand when the path feels unfamiliar? Can you trust that He is shaping something purposeful through the disruption?

As we begin this new theme on organizational change, this week invites you to reframe how you view transition. Instead of asking, "Why is this happening?" consider asking, "What is God doing through this?" Faithful leadership means remaining steady in uncertainty, seeking clarity through prayer, and staying anchored in trust even when outcomes remain unclear. Change may not always feel comfortable, but it often carries the seeds of something new, necessary, and divinely orchestrated.

Leadership Wisdom for the Christian Leader

Sometimes the hardest part of leadership is recognizing when a familiar path has reached its limit. What once felt stable begins to weaken. Participation fades. Energy shifts. Doors that once opened easily now resist. Many leaders try to force the past to function in the present, hoping old strategies will regain their strength. Yet some of the most significant breakthroughs begin when a leader admits that the landscape has changed and that God may be inviting them into something new.

Isaiah 43:19 offers a powerful reminder that God often works beyond our expectations. He makes streams in wastelands and roads through places that once felt impossible to cross. Leaders who embrace this truth learn not to interpret disruption as defeat. Instead, they respond with discernment, curiosity, and dependence on God's direction. When circumstances shift, God may be developing a leader's sight to recognize opportunities that comfort once concealed.

Not every change feels welcome, but that does not mean it lacks divine purpose. Jesus consistently invited people to leave behind what was familiar and follow Him into what was unknown. He challenged traditions, shifted mindsets, and reoriented values toward the Kingdom of God. He did not just change situations. He transformed perspectives.

Faithful leadership recognizes that obedience often requires releasing methods while preserving mission. Leaders must hold the mission tightly and the methods loosely. When leaders move forward with faith in uncertain seasons, they often discover impact that exceeds what old models could produce. What feels like disruption becomes transformation. What appears to be loss becomes expansion. God makes a way when leaders perceive His work and choose to walk with Him into what comes next.

Weekly Practice in Faith

We must remember that without change, nothing new can emerge. A seed cannot become a flower without transformation. A caterpillar cannot become a butterfly without experiencing metamorphosis. A child cannot grow into an adult without years of development. In the same way, the Israelites could not reach the Promised Land without embracing change, enduring transition, and trusting God through the process.

Whether change is planned or unexpected, whether it involves transition or deep transformation, we can take comfort knowing that God holds authority over all things, including time and change. He knows the outcome even when we do not. As we are reminded in Psalm 32:8, "I will instruct you and teach you in the way you should go; I will counsel you and watch over you."

This week, reflect on an area of change currently unfolding in your life or leadership. Let your leadership be rooted not in control, but in conviction. Just as Jesus remained faithful to His mission through opposition and disruption, strive to remain anchored in who you are and whose you are as change continues to unfold.

Time for Reflection

Take a quiet moment to consider the changes you are currently facing, personally, professionally, or within your organization. Isaiah 43:19 invites you to shift your focus from what is familiar to what is forming. God's new work may not look like comfort, but it always carries purpose.

What "new thing" might God be doing in your leadership right now? Pray for discernment to perceive it, courage to embrace it, and wisdom to lead through it with trust and clarity. Bring your thoughts before God and invite Him to shape you into a leader who brings peace and direction when everything around you feels unsettled.

Weekly Prayer

Lord, Change is not easy, and I often resist it, especially when I feel uncertain or out of control. But I know that You are constant, even when everything around me shifts. Teach me to trust Your purposes in seasons of disruption and to reflect Your integrity in how I respond. May my leadership bring clarity, peace, and hope to those I serve. Amen.

WEEK 22

Preparing for Change

"The plans of the diligent lead to profit
as surely as haste leads to poverty"

Proverbs 21:5 (NIV)

The Greek philosopher Heraclitus reminded us that change is not a matter of if but when. Wise leaders understand that outcomes are often determined long before change actually unfolds. Preparation is what turns chaos into clarity, anxiety into action, and uncertainty into direction.

Proverbs 21:5 gives a clear blueprint. The plans of the diligent lead to profit, while haste leads to poverty. Thoughtful preparation bears fruit. Rushed decisions cost more than time. They can erode trust, fragment teams, and weaken long-term mission.

As we continue exploring the theme of organizational change, this week's focus is simple but essential: slow down, prepare well, and lead forward with clarity. Change handled in haste becomes pressure. Change handled with diligence becomes transformation.

Leadership Wisdom for the Christian Leader

Some leaders make decisions out of urgency. For example, a new trend surfaces, a competitor moves in, or pressure descends from above, and suddenly leaders feel compelled to shift everything into overdrive. But wise leaders take a different approach. They pause long enough to understand what is at stake, ask the right questions, and prepare their people for what lies ahead. Their pace may appear slow, but their outcomes speak for themselves. Careful preparation often makes the difference between lasting success and frantic recovery.

Leaders are often tempted to rush change out of fear, pressure, or the desire to appear decisive. But meaningful change is rarely instant. It moves through stages: awareness, alignment, commitment, and action. Skipping preparation short-circuits the entire process. When leaders slow down to prepare, they create space for understanding, ownership, and smoother transitions, even in uncertain seasons.

Proverbs 21:5 reminds us that diligence is not perfectionism. It is stewardship. Preparing for change goes beyond timelines and task lists. It involves preparing hearts, clarifying purpose, anticipating resistance, and strengthening both emotional and spiritual readiness.

Jesus modeled this pattern with His disciples. He did not announce sudden shifts without preparation. He taught them, corrected them, walked with them, and then commissioned them. His leadership was deliberate, relational, and anchored in purpose.

Diligent leaders do not move reactively. They take time to understand context, anticipate challenges, and align their teams. Their intentional pace creates stability because it honors both the process and the people involved. Haste may look productive in the moment, but it often produces confusion, rework, and avoidable stress.

Leadership grounded in diligence builds confidence. Teams respond differently when decisions are thoughtful rather than impulsive. Preparation reduces avoidable mistakes and strengthens morale. Leaders who choose diligence over panic reflect biblical wisdom and demonstrate that sustainability is more valuable than speed.

Weekly Practice in Faith

This week, focus on how you prepare yourself and others when facing change. Identify one area, at home, at work, or in ministry, where change is either underway or approaching. Instead of reacting quickly, pause and commit to preparing with prayerful intention.

Gather information. Seek wise counsel. Consider who will be affected and how you can support them through the process.

Ask God to help you approach this situation not just as a problem-solver, but as a steward. Faithful leadership means counting the cost, thinking long-term, and caring deeply for the people you lead.

Time for Reflection

Ask yourself: Am I preparing for change with diligence, or reacting to it with haste?

In seasons of transition, it is tempting to rush decisions just to relieve pressure and uncertainty. But Proverbs 21:5 reminds us that preparation rooted in wisdom produces outcomes that honor God and serve others well.

Reflect on an upcoming change in your leadership or life. Have you sought godly counsel? Created space for prayerful planning? Clarified your purpose? Examined your motives?

Preparing well is not about controlling the future. It is about stewarding the present. Trust that God will honor plans formed in faith rather than fear.

Weekly Prayer

Lord, as I face seasons of change and new decisions, help me not to rush or react out of fear or pressure. Teach me to pause, to plan, and to trust You with every detail. Give me the discipline to prepare well and the humility to seek wise counsel. Remind me that leadership does not sprint ahead blindly but walks forward with diligence, discernment, and faith. Shape my plans according to Your will, and give me the courage to follow them with clarity and grace. In Jesus' name, Amen.

WEEK 23

Change Can Be Difficult

"In this world you will have trouble.
But take heart! I have overcome the world."

John 16:33 (NIV)

As adults, we experience change constantly. The shifts we encounter, both positive and negative, can leave us feeling as if we are riding an emotional roller coaster at home and in the workplace. From an organizational perspective, change may look like a new policy, restructuring, downsizing, or a slow effort to reshape culture. Regardless of the type or complexity of change, our thoughts often trigger strong emotions. We may feel joy, fear, discouragement, resistance, anxiety, or anger. Change can touch some of the deepest parts of our identity, which is why it can be one of the most significant and impactful experiences we face.

Jesus was no stranger to difficult change. In John 16, as He prepared His disciples for His departure, He did not soften the reality they were about to face. He told them that trouble was coming, that their world would be shaken, and that grief would come before joy. Yet He also gave them hope: "Take heart! I have overcome the world." Their obedience was not built on comfort. It was built on confidence in Him.

Leaders who follow Christ are called to that same kind of obedience. Not passive compliance, but active, courageous faith in God's greater plan. This kind of obedience does not pretend that difficulty is easy. It acknowledges discomfort, brings it before God, and chooses to move forward anyway. Obedience during difficult change is rarely loud or dramatic. It often looks like steady, faithful steps in the right direction, trusting that God is at work in the tension, the anxious thoughts, and the waiting.

This week, you are invited to reflect on what it means to obey when change is hard. Not only to endure it, but to embrace it as part of God's refining process, one that stretches your leadership, matures your faith, and equips you to serve others with resilience and grace.

Leadership Wisdom for the Christian Leader

There are seasons in leadership when difficulty is not a sign that something is wrong, but a sign that something is being reshaped. New systems disrupt comfortable routines. Established patterns are challenged. Resistance surfaces as people struggle with what feels unfamiliar. In those moments, frustration and fatigue can weigh heavily on both leaders and teams. The temptation is to abandon the process or force quick fixes. Yet transformation often passes through turbulence before it produces fruit. How leaders respond in those moments determines whether their teams move forward or slide back.

John 16:33 reminds leaders that trouble is part of life, but so is hope. Jesus does not promise a trouble free path. He promises His presence and His victory. Leaders who embrace this truth learn to expect challenges without being undone by them. Obstacles do not mean that God has stepped away from the work. Instead, they become places where His strength, wisdom, and faithfulness can be seen. When leaders ground their confidence in Christ rather than in circumstances, they can walk through disruption with peace and conviction.

Perseverance becomes contagious when modeled with honesty and steadiness. Teams draw strength from leaders who acknowledge the struggle, remain anchored, and keep pointing back to the larger purpose. A calm presence builds trust. Thoughtful encouragement renews courage. A leader who stays the course, even when results are delayed or messy, sends a clear message that the mission still matters. When leaders take heart in Christ's victory, they bring resilience into the room. Trouble may be unavoidable, but leaders anchored in Jesus help their teams move through it with hope, courage, and unwavering purpose.

Weekly Practice in Faith

This week, face your challenges with the confidence that Christ has already secured the victory. When difficulties arise in your leadership, relationships, or decisions, pause before reacting. Remind yourself that trials are not evidence of God's absence, but opportunities for His strength to be visible through you.

Lean into your faith. Turn to Scripture, and invite the Lord to help you see clearly and respond wisely. When you feel overwhelmed by emotion and in need of truth, pray the words of Psalm 56:3–4: "When I am afraid, I put my trust in you. In God, whose word I praise, in God I trust; I shall not be afraid." Lead with a calm assurance that peace is not the absence of trouble, but the presence of Christ in the middle of it. As you model that steady faith, those around you will see that resilience in leadership flows from trust, not control.

Time for Reflection

Read John 16:33 and pause to consider Jesus' words. He does not promise a life free of trouble, but He does promise His presence and His victory in the midst of it. Difficult change often brings disappointment, fear, or grief, especially when you cannot see what God is doing. Yet this verse calls you to "take heart," not because you are strong enough, but because Jesus has already overcome what overwhelms you.

Ask yourself: In the face of difficult change, am I leaning on my own strength, or on Christ's victory? Am I trying to control outcomes, or am I surrendering the process to God in prayer? Invite the Holy Spirit to show you where you are striving in your own power and where He is inviting you to trust, obey, and rest in Him even as you lead others through uncertainty.

Weekly Prayer

Lord, change is hard. It unsettles what feels safe and demands more of me than I feel ready to give. But I know that You are the same yesterday, today, and forever, even when everything around me shifts. Help me to trust You when the path forward feels unclear. Remind me that Your plans are good, even when they stretch me. I surrender my fear, my resistance, and my desire for control. Lead me step by step, and I will follow. Amen.

WEEK 24

How to Navigate Change

"Whether you turn to the right or to the left, your ears will hear a voice behind you, saying, 'This is the way; walk in it'"

Isaiah 30:21 (NIV)

God designed the human brain with remarkable precision, and one of its key structures is the amygdala (pronounced uh-mig-duh-luh). This small, almond-shaped structure rests deep within the temporal lobe. While the amygdala has multiple roles, its primary function is to help us process and evaluate potential threats or danger. When it senses a perceived threat, such as an unfamiliar change at work or within the organization, it triggers the release of stress hormones like cortisol and adrenaline. This hormonal surge is the direct cause of feelings like fear, anxiety, and resistance in the face of the unknown. This is why even positive change can feel disruptive. It is not immaturity, laziness, or stubbornness; it is biology.

Understanding this helps leaders recognize why people ask questions like, *Why change? Why now? How will this affect me?* When change surfaces, people do not first need more information. They need guidance. They need presence, patience, and a leader who understands how to shepherd people through uncertainty, not push them through it.

This week invites you to reflect on how you walk with people during times of transition. Are you rushing ahead alone? Or are you slowing down to guide your team with discernment and empathy? The most faithful leadership during change does not come from being forceful or fast, but from being aligned with God's direction and attentive to those you serve.

Leadership Wisdom for the Christian Leader
Leadership can feel like navigating through fog—pressure rising, expectations shifting, and clarity hard to find. In moments like these, followers do not simply need decisions; they need discernment. They need a leader who slows down long enough to listen, first to God, then to the people affected by the change.

Isaiah 30:21 gives a powerful image of spiritual leadership: God's voice coming from behind, guiding step by step, not through fear or urgency, but through steady clarity. This picture reminds leaders that guidance is always available. Even when the path is unfamiliar, God speaks into our uncertainty with direction and reassurance.

Leaders who walk closely with God learn to recognize His subtle cues nudges toward compassion, checks in the spirit, unexpected clarity during prayer, or a conviction that rises above emotion. This kind of guidance shifts leadership from reactive to rooted. When decisions are shaped by God's voice instead of pressure, they produce health, not harm. They lead people, not push them.

Spirit-led leadership restores confidence because it reflects God's character. People sense when a leader is making decisions from prayer rather than panic. They feel safer, more valued, and more hopeful. When leaders choose discernment over impulse, they cultivate a culture where confusion fades and clarity grows. Trust increases. Anxiety lessens. Direction returns. And teams find themselves walking in the path God has prepared.

Weekly Practice in Faith

This week, take intentional time to consider the influence your leadership has on others in moments of change. Begin with prayer: "Lord, help me notice what others are carrying, not just what needs to be done."

Then, identify one area in your leadership where change is necessary; perhaps communication, decision-making pace, or how you invite input. Take one small, concrete step toward navigating that change well:

- Schedule a conversation with someone affected.

- Ask for feedback before deciding.

- Slow down and prayerfully discern before acting.

- Invite wise counsel, remembering Proverbs 15:22: *"Plans fail for lack of counsel, but with many advisers they succeed."*

Lead through change not by pressure, but by presence, patience, and prayer.

Time for Reflection

Change often pressures leaders to act quickly, but Isaiah 30:21 reminds us that God's voice is steady, present, and guiding. Reflect on this question:

Did my last major leadership decision come from pressure or from prayer?

Consider whether you paused long enough to seek God's voice. Did you ask for discernment? Did you listen to those affected? Did you create space for clarity?

Ask God to reshape your posture so your leadership reflects His calm direction, even when everything around you feels unsettled.

Weekly Prayer

Lord, You are the One who goes before me, even when the road ahead feels uncertain. As I lead through change, help me quiet the noise so I can clearly hear Your voice. Give me wisdom to recognize when change is needed and courage to guide others with grace and steadiness. When I feel unsure, remind me that You are near, inviting me to walk in the way You have prepared. Help me lead with discernment, humility, and deep trust in Your direction. In Jesus' name, Amen.

WEEK 25

Careful, Change Can Transform Culture

"Therefore, my dear brothers and sisters, stand firm.

Let nothing move you."

1 Corinthians 15:58 (NIV)

Culture is one of the most precious elements of an organization. It shapes how people make sense, speak, serve, collaborate, and carry the mission. But culture is also fragile. It can be strengthened by change or quietly weakened by it. And more often than not, the difference is leadership.

Change tests what an organization truly believes. It pressures communication, exposes insecurities, and stretches relationships. Even positive change can shake the environment if the pace is too fast or the purpose is unclear. That is why Paul's words in 1 Corinthians 15:58 are so essential: *stand firm*. Change may shift systems, but culture must remain rooted in what is true, what is biblical, and what reflects Christ.

Jesus demonstrated this beautifully. Whether crowds followed Him or rejected Him, whether He taught on mountainsides or at dinner tables, His character never changed. He protected the "culture" of the Kingdom, modeling truth, compassion, courage, and humility no matter the circumstance.

This week invites you to reflect on this truth: change does not destroy culture; leaders do, when they stop guarding it. And likewise, leaders can strengthen culture when they choose steadiness, presence, and clarity in seasons of transition.

Leadership Wisdom for the Christian Leader

Every season of change contains risk, but the biggest risk is not the new structure, policy, or strategy. The biggest risk is the slow erosion of culture. When leaders rush toward change without stewardship, teams begin to feel unsettled, disconnected, or distrustful. Values get blurry. Communication becomes rushed. Pressure replaces purpose. Expectations shift but clarity does not.

Scripture warns leaders not to be moved by every shifting moment but to remain steady, grounded, and firm. *Stand firm. Let nothing move you.* This does not mean resisting change. It means protecting the culture while guiding the change.

Healthy leaders do this intentionally by:

- Clarifying values before outlining new plans
- Communicating purpose rather than simply announcing updates
- Checking the emotional temperature of the team, not just the timeline
- Protecting people from unnecessary chaos
- Aligning decisions with mission rather than pressure
- Modeling steadiness, especially when others feel unsure

Jesus did this with His disciples as He prepared them for major change: the cross, resurrection, and their future mission. He taught them. He prayed with them. He reassured them. He aligned their values before their assignment. He built culture before handing out responsibility.

Change will reshape processes, but leaders shape culture. And when leaders guard it, teams stay unified, grounded, and mission-focused; even when everything around them is shifting.

Weekly Practice in Faith

This week, choose one core cultural value that matters most to your team, household, ministry, or workplace. Examples include:

- Unity
- Respect
- Encouragement
- Integrity
- Service
- Healthy communication
- Excellence

Then:

1. Define it clearly: Write one sentence describing what this value *looks like* in daily behavior.

2. Assess it honestly: Has recent change weakened or strengthened this value?

3. Strengthen it intentionally: Choose one action this week that reinforces that value—both personally and publicly.

Strong cultures do not survive by accident. They survive because leaders protect what matters.

Time for Reflection

Culture mirrors the heart of leadership.

If the leader becomes anxious, the culture becomes anxious.

If the leader becomes reactive, the culture becomes fragile.

If the leader remains grounded, the culture becomes resilient.

Reflect on these questions:

- What part of your culture feels most fragile right now?
- Has change made you more grounded—or more reactive?
- Are you protecting values or only protecting tasks?
- How is God inviting you to "stand firm" in this season?

Ask God to give you clarity about what must stay firm even as new changes unfold.

Weekly Prayer

Lord, help me protect what matters most in the places I lead. Give me wisdom to know what must remain steady and what can change. Let my leadership reflect Your consistency, Your peace, and Your purpose. As I guide others, help me guard the culture You've entrusted to me. Teach me to lead with steadiness, humility, and courage so that the people I serve experience unity and strength, even in seasons of transition. Amen.

Leadership and the Cross

PROBLEM-SOLVING AND DECISION-MAKING

Weeks 26 - 30

Leadership inevitably brings moments when clear answers feel out of reach, and decisions carry weight that impacts more than just outcomes—they shape people, direction, and purpose. In these moments, leaders must slow down, seek God's wisdom, and act with faith over fear. The devotionals in the weeks ahead will walk you through this process: listening for divine wisdom in quiet moments, staying faithful under pressure, leading while surrendering control, and finding peace even when answers are unclear. True leadership is not about having all the solutions, but about knowing where to turn when you don't.

WEEK 26

Seek Wisdom in the Quite Hours

"If any of you lacks wisdom, you should ask God, who gives generously to all without finding fault, and it will be given to you."

James 1:5 (NIV)

Have you ever woken with a sudden moment of clarity? A problem that felt overwhelming the night before suddenly seems manageable in the morning light. This is not coincidence. Scripture teaches that God often works in the stillness of night to give His people understanding, peace, and direction.

James 1:5 invites us to ask God for wisdom whenever we lack it. He does not criticize us for asking. He gives generously and faithfully. That promise is not limited to our busy waking hours. Throughout Scripture, God speaks in dreams and night visions. Joseph received direction for his future while sleeping. Daniel received divine clarity about nations and kingdoms. The quiet hours often became the canvas for God's guidance.

God understands the weight leaders carry. During the busyness of the day, we may be too distracted or drained to hear Him clearly. But in sleep, when our striving settles and our minds are quiet, He often whispers answers, nudges our spirit, or plants seeds of clarity that rise with the morning. As leaders, we can easily rely on strategy, planning, and intellect to solve complex problems. Yet what we truly need is insight from God. That insight often comes in the quiet.

This week, do not overlook the wisdom God may reveal in stillness. Ask for His guidance before you sleep. Keep a journal nearby. Pay attention to the impressions that emerge when your heart is calm. Some of the most transformational insights may not come in noise or urgency but in the sacred quiet of the night.

Leadership Wisdom for the Christian Leader

There are moments in leadership when every option has been explored, every meeting has been held, and every logical approach has been exhausted. Pressure mounts. The path forward feels blocked. These moments remind leaders that human effort cannot substitute for divine clarity.

James 1:5 assures leaders that when they lack wisdom, they can ask God who gives generously without hesitation. This promise invites leaders to shift from self-reliance to spiritual dependence. Godly wisdom is not clever strategy or quick solutions. It is insight that aligns decisions with God's purpose and reveals possibilities that human reasoning may overlook.

Leaders who seek God's direction often discover that clarity arrives in simple but profound ways: a quiet moment that brings peace, a renewed mindset after rest, or an idea that surfaces when the noise settles. Wisdom often emerges when leaders are willing to slow down enough to listen.

Godly leadership begins with humility. It requires acknowledging that we do not see the entire picture. When leaders bring their challenges before God and ask for His wisdom, they model dependence rather than pride. That posture shapes character, deepens trust, and strengthens influence.

Leadership anchored in God's wisdom produces decisions that reflect faith, humility, and discernment. Teams trust leaders who acknowledge their limits and seek guidance beyond themselves.

When leaders listen for God's voice, they lead with clarity rooted not in their own insight but in God's provision. This creates healthy teams, opens new paths, and reveals solutions shaped by both stewardship and faith.

Weekly Practice in Faith

This week, take intentional time each evening to pause and ask God for wisdom regarding a challenge you are facing. Write down your specific question in a journal. Pray with expectation that God will respond in His timing.

As you sleep, remain open to insights, dreams, or renewed clarity that may come. In the morning, revisit what you recorded and note anything God brings to mind. Practice this for five nights. Pay attention to how God shapes your character during this process. True problem solving is not only about receiving answers. It is about becoming a leader prepared to steward them.

Time for Reflection

Read James 1:5 again. Take a few quiet moments to reflect on the questions you bring before God. Are they rooted in humility, or shaped by urgency and fear? Think about a time when God gave you clarity in an unexpected way. Was your heart ready to receive it?

Ask God to quiet your spirit, sharpen your insight, and prepare you to hear His guidance. What might God be revealing to you in this season, and are you still enough to receive it?

Weekly Prayer

Lord, You are the source of all wisdom. Thank You for being near when life's questions weigh heavily on my heart. When I do not know what to do, remind me that I can come to You without hesitation. Teach me to ask with faith, to wait with patience, and to listen with a quiet spirit. Shape me into a leader who seeks Your understanding above my own. In Jesus' name, Amen.

WEEK 27

Leaders Should Remain Faithful Under Pressure

"We must go through many hardships to enter the kingdom of God."

Acts 14:22 (NIV)

Leadership naturally brings seasons of pressure, moments when responsibility feels heavy and decisions carry significant weight. A single choice can influence the future of a team, the direction of an organization, or the well-being of people who depend on you. In those moments, strength is not found in titles, experience, or quick fixes. It is found in obedience to God, steady dependence on His wisdom, and the courage to keep moving even when the way forward is unclear.

Acts 14:22 reminds us that hardship is not an accident in the Christian life. "We must go through many hardships to enter the kingdom of God." Trials are not punishments or signs of spiritual failure. They are moments that shape a leader's faith, deepen their resilience, and refine their character. God does not leave leaders stranded in these hard seasons. He equips, strengthens, and guides those who seek Him.

This week invites you to examine how you respond when stress rises. Do you seek God before acting? Do you pause long enough to ask for His direction? Faithful leadership is not marked by perfection, but by steady obedience in the middle of pressure.

Leadership Wisdom for the Christian Leader

Some challenges arrive with such speed and intensity that they shake the confidence of even the strongest leaders. Systems break down. Emotions escalate. Criticism replaces encouragement. In these moments, leadership becomes less about managing tasks and more about staying grounded. Pressure has a way of revealing what a leader truly depends on. It exposes whether confidence comes from personal ability or from faith in God's sustaining presence.

Acts 14:22 reminds us that hardship is woven into the Christian journey. Faithful leadership does not avoid difficulty. It grows through it. Leaders who trust God in moments of pressure discover a strength beyond their own. Their clarity does not come from having all the answers, but from knowing the One who holds the outcome. Hard seasons refine leaders, stretching their patience, deepening their humility, and strengthening their spiritual maturity.

Scripture is full of leaders who faced pressure with faith. Moses stood before Pharaoh. Nehemiah rebuilt under constant opposition. Esther risked her life for her people. Jesus carried the weight of redemption itself. In each case, leadership under pressure required obedience to God's direction, not reliance on personal comfort.

When leaders remain steady, prayerful, and honest in difficult seasons, it strengthens the entire team. People draw confidence from a leader who maintains integrity when circumstances shake. Pressure becomes a place where trust grows, not where it collapses. Leadership anchored in Christ turns hardship into transformation for both the leader and those they serve.

Weekly Practice in Faith

This week, reflect intentionally on the weight of your responsibilities and how you carry them during seasons of pressure. Begin each morning with a simple prayer asking God for clarity, wisdom, and the strength to lead with integrity. Invite Him into every decision you face. When tension rises, pause before responding and ask, "Am I owning this moment with faith and obedience?"

Take one meaningful step each day that aligns with what you sense God is asking of you. This may mean addressing a long-avoided issue, offering needed encouragement, or engaging a difficult conversation with honesty and grace.

Time for Reflection

Acts 14:22 reminds us that hardship is not the exception in leadership, it is part of the journey. Pressure has a way of revealing what we truly trust, what fears still grip us, and where our obedience begins to waver. Take a quiet moment and reflect honestly:

> **Where are you feeling pressure right now?**
> Is it a decision you've been delaying, a conflict you're trying to avoid, or a responsibility that weighs heavier than usual? Pressure has a voice. Sometimes it whispers insecurity. Other times it shouts urgency. Listen long enough to discern what it is stirring in you.
>
> **What is this hardship exposing about your faith?**
> Does pressure push you toward prayer or toward panic? Does it stir humility, or does it awaken old habits of trying to control outcomes?
> God often uses pressure to reveal the gap between what we *say* we trust and what we *actually* depend on.
>
> **How are you responding to those who look to you for direction?**
> People often follow a leader's tone long before they follow a leader's plan. Your calmness, honesty, and steadiness may be the reassurance someone else desperately needs. Ask yourself:
> Are you leading from fear, fatigue, or faith?

Recall a time when God strengthened you through difficulty.
When did He show up in a moment when you felt outmatched or overwhelmed?
What did that season teach you about His character?
Pressure has a way of making us forget God's past faithfulness. Take time to remember it.

Now consider what God might be shaping in you through this current challenge.
Is He stretching your courage?
Is He training you to listen more closely?
Is He teaching you to trust Him with outcomes beyond your control?
Hardship becomes holy when it forms Christlike character within us.

Close this reflection by surrendering the pressure you feel.

Say to Him, "Lord, this moment is Yours. Shape me, steady me, and lead me through it.

Weekly Prayer
Lord, You see the responsibilities I carry and the pressures I feel. When I am overwhelmed, remind me that I do not lead alone. Give me wisdom to choose what is right, strength to stand firm in hardship, and courage to honor You in every decision. Help me carry my responsibilities with faith, integrity, and humility. In Jesus' name, Amen.

WEEK 28

Leaders Must Surrender to God's Wisdom

"Those who trust in themselves are fools,

but those who walk in wisdom are kept safe."

Proverbs 28:26 (NIV)

Every problem a leader faces becomes a crossroads between self-reliance and surrender. Some decisions feel routine, while others carry consequences that shape people, culture, and direction. Scripture is full of examples that warn against elevating personal logic over obedience to God, and few are more sobering than Judas Iscariot.

Judas was not an outsider or a casual follower. He walked with Jesus, served alongside the disciples, and held responsibility that reflected trust. Yet beneath the surface, small compromises were forming. His private choices ultimately led to a devastating act of betrayal. While Jesus' crucifixion fulfilled God's redemptive plan, Judas' decisions reveal what can unfold when leaders trust themselves more than they trust God.

Proverbs 28:26 draws a clear line: when leaders rely solely on their own judgment, they drift toward danger; when they walk in God's wisdom, they remain grounded, protected, and guided. Modern leaders face choices every day that tempt them to pursue convenience, control, or short-term gain. But godly leadership is rooted in surrender. When leaders seek wisdom from God, He provides clarity and direction that far surpass human insight.

This week calls leaders to evaluate not only what decisions they make, but how they make them. Wisdom begins with obedience. Impact begins with alignment.

Leadership Wisdom for the Christian Leader

Leadership can present decisions that appear straightforward on the surface but carry hidden complexity beneath. Pressure from time, expectations, or competing voices can lure leaders into shortcuts or compromises that seem harmless in the moment. Yet wisdom rarely moves at the pace of impulse. It requires space to pause, discern, and listen.

Proverbs 28:26 reminds leaders that self-confidence without God becomes a trap. It narrows vision and breeds a false sense of control. Leaders who rely on instinct alone eventually discover that intuition without obedience leads to inconsistency and avoidable mistakes. In contrast, those who walk in wisdom learn to seek God before acting.

They evaluate motives, consider long-term impact, and invite counsel rooted in truth.

Conviction-driven leadership often requires choosing the harder path. It may mean delaying a decision to pray, pursuing clarity instead of speed, or rejecting options that promise quick results but compromise integrity. Wisdom is not measured by how fast a leader solves problems, but by how faithfully they align their decisions with God's character.

Wise leaders cultivate a culture of stability. Their decisions strengthen trust, reinforce integrity, and model maturity. As they lead from a place of surrender rather than pride, God equips them with insight that protects their mission, people, and witness. Anchored in His wisdom, they lead with clarity that withstands pressure and creates lasting impact.

Weekly Practice in Faith

This week, take time to evaluate the rhythm of your decision-making. Notice whether your choices flow from prayerful dependence or from urgency, pressure, or habit. Begin each day by asking God for discernment. Invite Him to guide not only major decisions but small ones that shape your influence.

Choose one decision you will face this week and intentionally slow down the process. Seek God's guidance through prayer. Consult Scripture. Invite counsel from a spiritually mature voice. Allow the

Lord to reveal not just what to do, but how to approach it with humility and integrity.

Responsible leadership is built on consistent surrender, not occasional moments of desperation. Practice walking in wisdom daily and allow God to shape the leader you are becoming.

Time for Reflection

Leadership often creates the illusion that answers must come quickly and confidently. But wisdom rarely emerges from pressure; it grows within leaders who embrace humility and slow down long enough to seek God. As you reflect on your recent decisions, consider the posture of your heart in those moments. Many leaders discover that the greatest challenge is not finding the right answer, but releasing the instinct to depend on themselves.

Pay attention to the internal pull toward urgency or self-assurance. Self-reliance tends to produce strain and narrow thinking, while godly wisdom brings steadiness and deeper clarity. Reflect on the moments in your leadership when slowing down produced better outcomes, stronger relationships, or surprising peace. Let those memories remind you that wisdom is not passive; it is intentional.

This week, create space for reflection that realigns your heart with God's direction. Allow His presence to steady you. Let His wisdom reshape your thinking. Leadership anchored in surrender becomes leadership that endures.

Weekly Prayer

Lord, guard my heart from the temptation to rely on my own understanding. Teach me to seek Your counsel in every decision, whether large or small. When pressures rise, steady me with Your wisdom. Help me choose obedience over convenience and trust over control. Shape my leadership according to Your truth and guide my steps with clarity and peace. In Jesus' name, Amen.

WEEK 29

When Answers are Hard to Find

"God is our refuge and strength, a very present help in trouble."

Psalm 46:1 (NIV)

Every leader eventually encounters moments when solutions seem to evaporate. Meetings produce no clarity. Advice feels repetitive. Strategies stall. You pray, reflect, analyze, and still feel as if you're standing at a crossroads without a sign. These seasons can be exhausting, especially for leaders who are used to bringing direction and stability to others.

Yet Scripture reminds us that God is fully present in the silence, the strain, and the uncertainty. Figures like Job, Joseph, Daniel, and David faced seasons where answers did not come quickly. They endured long stretches of tension where God seemed quiet, yet He was actively shaping their strength, character, and faith. Psalm 46:1 declares that God is "a very present help in trouble," not distant, not delayed, but present.

This week focuses on the kind of leadership that doesn't crumble when clarity is missing. Instead of grasping for instant answers, faithful leaders learn to stand firm in God's presence, trusting that He will guide them in due time.

Leadership Wisdom for the Christian Leader

Leadership can sometimes feel like walking through haze. You know you must keep moving, but the path ahead is blurred by pressure, complexity, or emotional weight. It is in these moments that leaders rediscover where their true strength comes from. God never intended for leaders to solve every problem through personal skill alone. He calls them to lean on Him, especially when the moment feels bigger than their capacity.

Psalm 46:1 anchors leaders in a profound truth: God is both refuge and strength. He provides safety when uncertainty rises and power when exhaustion sets in. Leaders who cling to this truth respond to challenges differently. They do not panic when answers delay. They do not abandon their calling when pressure escalates. Instead, their posture becomes steady, grounded, and deeply rooted in dependence on God.

When leaders operate from this place of refuge, their presence becomes a source of stability for everyone around them. They bring calm to anxious teams and hope to discouraged hearts.

People begin to notice that their leadership is not driven by self-preservation but by servant-hearted strength.

Over time, this steady posture transforms the culture of a team. Stability spreads. Trust is renewed. Courage becomes contagious. Leaders who anchor themselves in God's presence create environments where people can breathe again, think clearly, and find strength to persevere. God does not promise quick answers. He promises Himself. Leaders who embrace this truth experience resilience that cannot be manufactured and peace that cannot be explained apart from Him.

Weekly Practice of Faith

This week, commit to leading from a place of refuge rather than urgency. Identify one situation that has been weighing heavily on you. Instead of striving for immediate resolution, bring it before God each morning in prayer. Name it honestly. Surrender your need to control the outcome. Ask the Lord to steady your heart before you take even a single step.

Throughout the week, when tension rises, pause for a brief moment of silence. Remind yourself that God is present in that very moment. As you lead others, let your words and actions reflect calm confidence rather than pressure. Let your presence model the strength that comes from leaning on the Lord, not from finding the perfect answer.

Time for Reflection

There are moments in leadership when the path ahead refuses to reveal itself. The instinct may be to push harder, to force solutions, or to mask uncertainty with confidence. But spiritual maturity grows when leaders learn to rest in God's presence even before clarity arrives.

Take time this week to reflect on where you have been relying too heavily on your own strength. Notice the places where frustration, fatigue, or fear have crept in. These are often signals that your heart is carrying more than it was meant to bear. As you reflect, allow God to reorient your spirit toward His promises. Strength comes from abiding. Peace flows from His nearness. Vision returns when the soul grows still enough to hear His voice.

When leaders allow God to meet them in the quiet tension between problem and solution, they discover a deeper resilience; one shaped not by answers, but by relationship.

Weekly Prayer

Lord, when I feel overwhelmed and do not know what to do, help me to remember that You are my refuge and strength. Remind me that I do not need to have all the answers in order to lead with love. Use me as a steady hand and a calm voice when the people around me need assurance. Thank You for being near in every moment. Amen

WEEK 30

Leaders, Remember! God will Deliver and Answer

"The righteous person may have many troubles,

But the Lord delivers him from them all."

Psalm 34:19 (NIV)

Leadership often asks more of us than we feel prepared to give. Decisions pile up, people depend on us, and problems press with a weight that grows heavier over time. Even the strongest leaders eventually reach moments when they feel worn thin, stretched to their limits, or unsure of how to move forward. Scripture never denies this reality. It tells us plainly that the righteous will face many troubles. Trouble is not a sign of failure. It is part of the journey.

What separates godly leaders from overwhelmed leaders is not the absence of pressure, but the presence of God in the midst of it.

Psalm 34:19 reminds us that God does not abandon His people when life becomes difficult. He is active, attentive, and deeply involved in the lives of those who trust Him. Deliverance is not a vague hope. It is a promise.

This week is an invitation to step out of self-reliance and into surrendered dependence. God strengthens, guides, and delivers those who call on Him. The weight you carry is not meant to be lifted alone.

Leadership Wisdom for the Christian Leader

Pressure reveals what a leader truly depends on. When solutions fail, when deadlines close in, or when resources fall short, leaders confront the limits of their own strength. These moments, though uncomfortable, become spiritual turning points. They expose whether a leader is leaning on personal ability or resting in the faithfulness of God.

Psalm 34:19 offers a grounding truth: trouble may be certain, but so is God's deliverance. Leaders who embrace this promise stop striving to control every outcome. Their focus shifts from managing pressure to trusting the One who sustains them through it. This surrender is not passivity. It is wisdom. It frees leaders from the exhausting belief that everything depends on them.

God's deliverance often unfolds quietly, through renewed strength, fresh clarity, unexpected provision, or the right voice arriving at the right moment. Leaders who place their confidence in Him develop a calm resilience that stands out in times of tension. Their leadership becomes a steadying force. They inspire courage not by pretending to have every answer, but by modeling trust in the God who does.

As this posture takes root, it influences team culture. People feel safer. Trust deepens. Fear diminishes. The presence of a faith-anchored leader elevates the environment in ways strategy alone never can. Leaders who trust God's deliverance guide others into hope rather than panic, clarity rather than confusion, and endurance rather than collapse.

Weekly Practice in Faith

This week, identify one area of leadership where pressure has been building. Instead of rushing to solve it, begin by surrendering it. Write the situation down, acknowledge the weight it carries, and invite God into every layer of it. Pray not only for a solution but for strength, clarity, and calm as you wait.

Throughout the week, practice leading with a spirit of dependence. Before important conversations or decisions, pause for a brief prayer. Center your focus on God as your source of wisdom, not on your ability to manage the moment. As pressure arises, let your response reflect trust rather than urgency. Let your pace be guided by peace rather than fear.

Time for Reflection

The promise of Psalm 34:19 invites leaders to rest in God's faithfulness, even when trouble feels overwhelming. Reflect on where you have been carrying responsibilities alone. Notice the places where exhaustion, frustration, or discouragement have settled into your leadership. These may be signs that your heart has drifted toward self-reliance.

Allow God to bring your attention back to His deliverance. His presence is not symbolic. It is sustaining. Strength often arrives not when the situation changes, but when the leader's posture does. As you reflect, consider the quiet ways God has delivered you in the past. Remember the times when His provision arrived unexpectedly or His timing proved wiser than your own. These memories become anchors that stabilize your faith in the present.

Leadership is not measured by the absence of trouble but by the depth of trust you carry through it.

Weekly Prayer

Lord, I come to You today acknowledging that my strength is limited, but Yours is not. Teach me to trust You more fully, especially when the path is unclear or the problem feels overwhelming. In Jesus' name, Amen

Leadership and the Cross

CONFLICT MANAGEMENT

> **Weeks 31 - 35**
>
> Conflict is inevitable, but as leaders, how we respond to it defines our influence. Some leaders avoid conflict, others try to control it, but Christlike leadership approaches it with wisdom, empathy, and truth. In the weeks ahead, you'll reflect on five biblical approaches to managing conflict with character. You'll explore what it means to Lead by Understanding, to act as a Peacemaker, to Guide Others to Common Ground, to Build Stronger Relationships, and to Lead with Fairness and Justice. Each devotion invites you to face tension not as a threat, but as a chance to grow, restore, and lead with integrity.

WEEK 31

In Moments of Conflict, Lead by Understanding

"Let us therefore make every effort to do what leads to peace and to mutual edification."

Romans 14:19 (NIV)

Conflict is an unavoidable part of leadership. It can rise from miscommunication, personality differences, unspoken expectations, or competing priorities. Yet how a leader responds in those moments reveals more about their character than their competence. Some leaders attempt to force a solution. Others avoid conflict entirely, hoping time will fix what tension has created. Christ centered leadership, however, calls us to a deeper posture: understanding.

Understanding does not require agreement, nor does it mean abandoning truth. It means slowing down long enough to listen, seeking context before forming conclusions, and honoring the person even when their perspective challenges our own. This approach requires patience, humility, and discipline. It reflects a leader who values people over control and clarity over assumptions.

Romans 14:19 calls leaders to pursue peace and to build others up. That pursuit begins with understanding, because no reconciliation can take root without it. When leaders embrace understanding as a foundation, conflict becomes an opportunity to strengthen relationships, deepen trust, and cultivate spiritual maturity. This week invites you to consider how understanding shapes your leadership, particularly in moments of tension, and how choosing peace builds character and influence.

Leadership Wisdom for the Christian Leader

Disagreement and friction can spread quickly through an organization. Misunderstandings deepen. Assumptions harden. Collaboration fades. In these moments, leaders must choose how they will show up. They can react with force, take sides, or rush to fix the issue. Or they can slow the pace and seek to understand the deeper story unfolding beneath the surface. Real peace rarely comes from pressure. It grows when a leader listens long enough to see the heart behind the conflict.

Romans 14:19 reminds leaders to pursue what builds up. True peace is not silence or avoidance. It is the presence of clarity, humility, and shared commitment. Leaders who seek understanding create safe environments for honest dialogue. They acknowledge concerns, clarify expectations, and affirm the value of every person at the table. They help others see that conflict is not a battlefield but a bridge, when approached with maturity and grace.

When understanding becomes part of the culture, trust takes root. Differences become opportunities for learning rather than barriers to unity. People feel respected even when they disagree. Leaders who model this form of Christlike leadership demonstrate that peace is the result of steady, disciplined choices, not accidental moments.

Weekly Practice in Faith

This week, choose one relationship or situation where conflict or misunderstanding has created distance. Write it down so it becomes something you intentionally address rather than avoid.

Each day, pray specifically for a heart that listens before it reacts. Ask God to help you see the situation through the other person's eyes. Then take one meaningful step toward restoring understanding. This might be asking a clarifying question, initiating a gentle conversation, or offering forgiveness where it is needed. Leadership often begins not with speaking, but with listening. When you seek understanding, you reflect the humility and patience of Christ.

Time for Reflection

Character driven leadership requires honesty with oneself. Conflict reveals the posture of the heart. Take a quiet moment to reflect on your patterns. Do you pursue peace, or do you unintentionally fuel tension? Do your responses lift others up, or do they protect your own viewpoint? Do you seek to understand, or do you expect others to understand you first?

Invite God to show you opportunities for growth. Pray for the wisdom to approach conflict with clarity and humility, and for the courage to prioritize understanding over the urge to be right.

Weekly Prayer

Lord, thank You for calling me to lead with a spirit of peace and a heart that seeks understanding. When conflict arises, help me listen with patience, respond with grace, and pursue unity with integrity. Make me a bridge where there is misunderstanding and a steady presence where there is tension. May my leadership strengthen others and reflect the character of Christ. In Jesus' name, Amen.

WEEK 32

In Moments of Conflict, Be the Peacemaker

"Blessed are the peacemakers,

for they shall be called sons of God."

Matthew 5:9 (NIV)

Conflict will surface in any workplace. Tension, disagreement, and disruption are not signs of poor leadership. They are signs of real people navigating real pressures. When conflict appears, leaders face a choice. They can react from pride or frustration, or they can step forward with intentional calm. Jesus honored those who choose the second path. Peacemakers do not hide from conflict. They step into the moment with a spirit that seeks restoration rather than victory.

Peacemaking requires courage, wisdom, and humility. It is active rather than passive. It listens before speaking, seeks understanding before judgment, and pursues a path that dignifies everyone involved. This week calls you to reflect on your own presence in moments of tension. In every setting you lead, your words and posture can either stir anxiety or cultivate peace. The invitation of Matthew 5:9 is clear. Christ calls His leaders to be instruments of reconciliation.

Leadership Wisdom for the Christian Leader

Leadership often requires stepping into messy and emotionally charged spaces. Teams may pull in different directions. Expectations collide. Pressure rises from above and below. In these moments, leaders discover that peacemaking is not about keeping everyone comfortable. It is about guiding people toward clarity and unity without sacrificing truth.

Matthew 5:9 reminds us that peacemakers reflect the heart of God. They do not resolve conflict by ignoring it. They do the harder work of bringing issues into the open with honesty and grace. Peacemakers hold themselves accountable for the tone they set. They refuse to let frustration dictate their approach. Instead, they create space for real conversation and shared understanding.

When leaders pursue peace with integrity, trust grows. Even difficult outcomes are easier to accept when people feel heard and respected. Peacemaking strengthens teams because it builds a culture where concerns are brought forward rather than hidden, and where collaboration becomes possible even in disagreement. This form of leadership is not fragile. It is deeply rooted in commitment to truth and the well-being of others. It reflects Christ, who always moved toward reconciliation, never away from it.

Weekly Practice in Faith

This week, identify one area where tension or misunderstanding has created distance in your leadership. Bring it specifically to God in prayer, asking for insight into how you can step forward as a peacemaker.

Reach out to someone affected by the situation and listen without defending, correcting, or offering solutions. Let your posture be one of curiosity and compassion. Write down what you learn from the interaction and how it may guide your next steps.

Remember that peacemaking is not a single action. It is a steady commitment to leading with truth, empathy, and clarity.

Time for Reflection

Peacemaking is not the absence of conflict. It is the willingness to enter conflict with a heart anchored in Christ. Take time today to consider whether any unresolved tension has lingered because it was easier to avoid it. Reflect on how your leadership might change if you approached these moments with patience, humility, and a genuine desire to restore peace.

Invite God to help you become a leader who brings healing rather than division, clarity rather than confusion, and unity rather than suspicion.

Weekly Prayer

Lord, thank You for the call to be a peacemaker. When conflict rises, help me respond with wisdom, patience, and compassion. Give me the courage to address tension instead of avoiding it, and the humility to listen well. Make my leadership a reflection of Your heart and let peace grow wherever You have placed me. In Jesus' name, Amen.

WEEK 33

In Moments of Conflict, Seek Common Ground

"Do nothing from selfish ambition or conceit, but in humility count others more significant than yourselves. Let each of you look not only to his own interests, but also to the interests of others."

Phillipians 2:3-4 (NIV)

Conflict s rarely about the issue alone. It often emerges from competing priorities, wounded pride, or assumptions formed long before the disagreement began. Leaders who guide others to common ground understand that unity does not require uniformity and agreement does not mean everyone receives their preferred outcome. At the core of reconciliation is a willingness to listen, empathize, and lay aside selfish ambition.

Whether the tension stems from team dynamics, partnerships, or competing visions, friction grows when people hold different values, expectations, or fears. In these moments, leaders carry the responsibility to seek understanding and create a shared path forward. Philippians 2:3-4 offers a clear foundation for this work, calling leaders to humility and to value the interests of others alongside their own. This is the beginning of common ground.

Finding common ground does not require leaders to dilute convictions or avoid difficult conversations. Instead, it calls them to cultivate an environment where clarity, respect, and mutual purpose can emerge. Leaders who listen first, extend grace, and prioritize unity over ego reflect the servant-hearted posture of Christ. Their humility shapes both the way they resolve conflict and the way they shepherd others through it.

This week invites you to reflect on how responsibility shows up in moments of tension. Healthy leadership seeks solutions that honor people, preserve dignity, and strengthen community.

Leadership Wisdom for the Christian Leader

Workplaces often become battlegrounds for ideas, identities, and expectations. When tensions rise, pride quickly becomes the obstacle that prevents people from hearing one another. Some leaders respond by forcing a decision. Others step back, hoping distance will dissolve the conflict. Yet wise leaders understand that humility is the key that transforms division into collaboration.

Philippians 2:3-4 calls leaders to reject selfish ambition and to genuinely consider the interests of others. This call does not silence conviction. It shapes posture. Humility strengthens a leader's ability to build unity because it removes the need to protect ego or defend preference. When leaders choose to listen carefully, speak truthfully, and honor the value of each person involved, they reflect the heart of Christ. They secure trust and create space for shared purpose.

Humility turns conflict into opportunity. When leaders approach disagreements with a spirit of service, they pull people toward understanding instead of pushing them toward sides. Teams begin to appreciate diverse perspectives and recognize the value each contributor brings. Leaders who embrace this passage cultivate cultures marked by respect, empathy, and collective strength. In such environments, relationships deepen, solutions improve, and the mission becomes stronger than individual preference. Humility is not weakness. It is spiritual clarity that strengthens leadership.

Weekly Practice in Faith

This week, identify one place where conflict or tension has disrupted unity in your team, organization, or relationships. Write it down as a point of focus in your journal.

Pray each day for the humility to listen well and for the discernment to seek common ground. Invite God to shape your tone and your approach. Then take one small step toward reconciliation. Initiate a conversation. Ask someone involved to share their perspective without interruption. Seek clarity where assumptions have taken root. Offer grace where frustration has built walls.

Remember that leadership is not about defending your position. It is about modeling the humility that opens the way for peace. When you take responsibility for creating understanding, you reflect the heart of Christ to those you lead.

Time for Reflection

Philippians 2:3-4 challenges leaders to resist pride, competition, and the instinct to protect personal preference. This passage calls for a different kind of leadership, one marked by empathy, humility, and shared purpose. These qualities do not arise automatically. They require intention and surrender.

Take time to reflect on your recent responses to conflict. Have you approached disagreements with humility, or have you allowed frustration to shape your posture? Have your decisions built unity, or have they unintentionally widened gaps?

Ask God to reveal where your leadership can become more peace-building. Allow Him to shape your heart so that the way you lead brings people together rather than pulling them apart.

Weekly Prayer

Lord, thank You for calling me to lead with humility and to pursue unity in moments of conflict. Shape my heart to reflect Yours. Give me ears that listen, words that heal, and a spirit that seeks understanding over pride. Teach me to value others and to guide them toward reconciliation with grace and wisdom. May my leadership bring honor to You and peace to those I serve. In Jesus' name, Amen.

WEEK 34

Lead by Building Relationships

"Bear with each other and forgive one another if any of you has a grievance against someone. Forgive as the Lord forgave you. And over all these virtues put on love, which binds them all together in perfect unity."

Colossians 3:13-14 (NIV)

Leaders are often recognized for their strategies, achievements, and decisive actions. Yet beneath every success lies a deeper truth: relationships sustain the work. Whether in families, teams, or organizations, the ability to cultivate healthy relationships is one of the most enduring strengths a leader can develop. Where relationships flourish, trust grows. Where trust grows, unity forms. And unity fuels collective impact.

Still, relationships can be challenging. People fall short. Expectations collide. Misunderstandings take root. Leaders are then faced with a choice. They can withdraw into self-protection or they can lean forward with grace, patience, and humility. Paul's words in Colossians remind us that Christian leadership is not merely about tolerating others. It is about bearing with one another, forgiving fully, and clothing ourselves in love. These actions demand spiritual maturity because they place the needs of people above personal comfort.

This week invites you to examine how you build, repair, and strengthen relationships. Leadership grounded in service chooses connection over convenience and grace over resentment. It mirrors the heart of Christ, who held people together through love that remained steady even when others faltered.

Leadership Wisdom for the Christian Leader

Workplaces often carry wounds that procedures and policies cannot fix. Miscommunication, unmet expectations, and hurt feelings can quietly fracture relationships long before performance suffers. When trust is bruised, leaders may feel pressure to move forward quickly, hoping time will heal what words have not addressed. Yet genuine restoration requires more. It requires leaders who are willing to stop, listen, and walk with people through discomfort rather than rushing past it.

Colossians 3:13-14 anchors leaders in a different way of responding. Bearing with one another calls for patience when others fall short. Forgiving as the Lord forgave calls for mercy even when wrongs feel personal. Clothing ourselves in love calls for intentional care that restores dignity. These practices shift leadership from task management to relational stewardship. Forgiveness does not erase accountability. It creates the space needed for healing to begin.

When leaders model grace consistently, the culture shifts. Trust slowly rebuilds. Conversations soften. People feel safe enough to name hurts and participate in solutions. Unity becomes more than a slogan because relationships are tended with care. Small actions like acknowledging pain, offering a sincere apology, or listening without defensiveness can repair fractures that once felt permanent. Leaders who carry the love of Christ into their relational decisions cultivate environments where connection is stronger than conflict and unity becomes possible again.

Weekly Practice in Faith

This week, identify one relationship in your life or leadership that needs attention, renewal, or intentional care. Ask God to show you what step is needed. It may be a difficult conversation, an apology you have avoided, or forgiveness you have withheld. It may be as simple as checking on someone who feels unseen or misunderstood.

Commit to one small act each day that strengthens relational trust. Listen more deeply. Slow down your response. Offer encouragement without being asked. Choose to serve rather than manage. As the week progresses, journal what changes you notice in your own heart. Leadership rooted in service grows stronger through small, faithful acts that honor others and reflect Christ.

Time for Reflection

Healthy relationships require leaders who are patient, gracious, and willing to forgive. People will disappoint or challenge you, and some conflicts may feel personal. Yet love and forgiveness are the threads that hold teams together when tension rises. Unity is not the absence of conflict. It is the decision to respond with humility and compassion.

Take time today to reflect on a relationship that needs healing or renewed understanding. Have you been slow to forgive or quick to judge? Have you withdrawn instead of leaning forward in love? Ask God to soften your heart and help you pursue reconciliation with wisdom. Let your leadership become a living picture of grace in action.

Weekly Prayer

Lord, Teach me how to serve others by prioritizing relationships, even when it feels inconvenient. Use me as an instrument of healing in broken relationships. Give me the courage to forgive, the strength to apologize, and the wisdom to build others up. May my actions reflect Your heart, and may I be known as a leader who values unity over ego. In Jesus' name, Amen.

WEEK 35

Be a Leader That is Just and Fair

"He has shown you, O mortal, what is good.

And what does the Lord require of you?

To act justly and to love mercy

and to walk humbly with your God."

Micah 6:8 (NIV)

Fairness is one of the clearest indicators of a leader's character. Titles may open doors and strategies may shape outcomes, but justice, mercy, and humility reveal who a leader truly is under pressure. When decisions carry weight and outcomes impact lives, a leader's commitment to fairness is tested. In these moments, fairness is not simply about equal treatment. It is about doing what is right, even when the cost is personal.

Micah 6:8 offers a straightforward and uncompromising blueprint. Acting justly reflects God's concern for dignity and truth. Loving mercy reflects His compassion for people who fall short. Walking humbly reflects a heart surrendered to God rather than pride or self protection. Leaders who embody these qualities stand firm when it is easier to compromise, and they lead with integrity when others choose convenience. This week invites you to reflect on fairness as a spiritual discipline, a visible expression of God's character through your leadership.

Leadership Wisdom for the Christian Leader

Leadership eventually brings a moment when the ethical choice is also the costly one. It may disrupt your plans, test relationships, or challenge the comfort of your organization. These defining moments separate leaders driven by personal advantage from leaders guided by godly conviction.

Micah 6:8 sets a standard that reaches beyond policy or procedure. Justice calls a leader to uphold what is right even when silence would be easier. Mercy asks a leader to show compassion when frustration or impatience feels justified. Humility reminds a leader that their authority is not a shield for self interest but a tool for serving others. Leaders who live by these values do not need applause to validate them. Their credibility grows naturally because their actions match their convictions.

Cultures shaped by justice and mercy reflect stability and trust. People feel safe bringing concerns forward because they know fairness is the rule rather than the exception. Even when difficult decisions must be made, teams respond differently when they see humility guiding the process. Ethical leadership becomes a testimony that God's character does not shift with pressure. Fairness becomes part of the culture, not because it is easy, but because one leader chose conviction over convenience.

Weekly Practice in Faith

Dedicate time this week to examine how fairness influences your leadership. Reflect honestly on whether your decisions are shaped more by comfort or by conviction. Consider situations where you may have overlooked inequity, avoided a hard conversation, or allowed convenience to guide your choices.

Choose one specific circumstance where fairness needs to be re-centered. Take a step toward addressing it with integrity. This could involve revisiting a past decision, advocating for someone marginalized, or correcting an imbalance that has gone unnoticed. Document what you do and ask God to shape your character through the process. Fairness is strengthened through practice, not avoidance.

Time for Reflection

Fair leadership requires courage, consistency, and a heart willing to serve rather than dominate. Conflict and tension often reveal the true motivations behind a leader's actions. Justice guards against favoritism. Mercy guards against harshness. Humility guards against pride. Together, they create a posture that honors God and strengthens the people you lead.

Spend time reflecting on a recent moment of conflict or tension. Consider the internal posture that guided your response. Allow God to reveal where justice, mercy, or humility needs to grow. Leadership shaped by these qualities brings healing to relationships and clarity to decision making. It becomes a quiet witness to God's character in a world desperate for fairness.

Weekly Prayer

Lord, thank You for showing me what is good and for calling me to a higher standard in my leadership. Strengthen my resolve to act justly, to love mercy, and to walk humbly with You. Give me courage to choose what is right even when it is costly and grace to lead with fairness in every decision. May my leadership reflect Your truth and inspire others to pursue justice with confidence and integrity. In Jesus' name, Amen.

A 52-Week Devotional for Leaders

Leadership and the Cross

MOTIVATING YOUR TEAM

Weeks 36 - 40

Great leadership is not just about setting direction, but about stirring hearts. Motivation fuels the energy and commitment that teams need to thrive, especially in challenging or uncertain times. In the weeks ahead, you'll explore how leaders can draw from a well of encouragement, compassion, and faith to uplift those they serve. You'll reflect on the power of motivation, the role of encouragement, the strength found in compassionate leadership, the spiritual drive that comes from faith, and the deep impact of timely recognition and affirmation. These practices don't just inspire action; they build loyalty, resilience, and trust in every corner of your team.

WEEK 36

Understand the Power of Motivation

"Let us not become weary in doing good, for at the proper time we will reap a harvest if we do not give up."

Galatians 6:9 (NIV)

Motivation is often treated as a quick spark, a moment of inspiration, or a leadership tactic. But lasting motivation grows from something deeper. It is nurtured by purpose, sustained by conviction, and strengthened by a leader's character. As Frederick Herzberg observed, "True motivation comes from achievement, personal growth, and the work itself." It is rooted in a sense of purpose and a belief that the work matters. Teams thrive when they believe their effort matters and when their leader reflects that belief through personal integrity and steady example.

For leaders, character becomes the anchor that fuels motivation. When you model perseverance, demonstrate consistency, and remain faithful in difficult moments, your team draws strength from your posture. People are encouraged not only by words, but by the visible testimony of a leader who refuses to give up. Galatians 6:9 reminds us that perseverance is not wasted. God honors faithfulness. This week is an invitation to evaluate how your character influences the motivation of those who follow you.

Leadership Wisdom for the Christian Leader

There are seasons when the emotional temperature of a team begins to drop. Fatigue shows up quietly in slower conversations, shorter patience, and the gradual loss of enthusiasm. It is in these moments that leadership carries its greatest weight. Some leaders push harder. Others shrink back. Wise leaders do something different. They offer perspective.

Galatians 6:9 provides that perspective. It speaks directly to teams that feel drained or discouraged and to leaders who are carrying more than they let on. The verse does not ignore the reality of weariness. Instead, it acknowledges it with honesty and then lifts the eyes of believers toward hope. Faithful work may feel tiring, but it is never empty. The harvest will come in God's timing, not ours.

Leaders who internalize this truth become steady anchors for their teams. They speak encouragement rooted in Scripture rather than empty positivity. They remind their people that meaningful work is often slow, challenging, and demanding. Yet God honors faithful commitment. When leaders reconnect their team to purpose, they restore clarity, resilience, and hope. Culture shifts when a leader holds firm, stays patient, and directs weary hearts back toward a mission worth pursuing.

Encouragement becomes a powerful ministry in the hands of a leader who refuses to give up. The harvest does not arrive through intensity. It arrives through steady faithfulness. When leaders embody perseverance and lift their teams with clarity and compassion, they help others discover strength they did not realize they possessed. A culture that once felt tired can become a culture marked by resilience, unity, and renewed purpose.

Weekly Practice in Faith

This week, take time to reflect on how your character influences the motivation of those around you. Consider the tone you set when challenges arise, the example you model when circumstances feel heavy, and the consistency you show when results are slow. Identify one practical way to demonstrate perseverance in a situation that is testing your patience. This might include recognizing someone's quiet effort, stepping into a difficult task without complaint, or reminding your team of the purpose behind the work. Let your actions speak hope into tired hearts.

Time for Reflection

Motivation grows in environments shaped by clarity, encouragement, and trust. Leaders who persevere with integrity do more than complete tasks. They nurture resilience in others. Galatians 6:9 offers a promise that faithful work carries eternal value, even when the visible harvest has not yet arrived.

Reflect on the individuals you lead. Consider who may be feeling overlooked, tired, or discouraged. Think about how your presence, posture, or perspective could help them recover strength. Ask God to renew your own motivation, so that you can serve as an example of steady faith. Leadership marked by character becomes a quiet testimony that God is at work even in slow seasons. Your consistency can be the reminder others need to keep going.

Weekly Prayer

Lord, thank You for the promise that faithful work is never wasted. Strengthen my character so that I can lead with perseverance and clarity, especially in difficult moments. Renew my motivation and use my actions and words to encourage those I lead. Help me to create a culture where purpose is clear and hope is restored. In Jesus' name, Amen.

WEEK 37

Be a Source of Great Encouragement

"And let us consider how we may spur one another on toward love and good deeds, not giving up meeting together; but encouraging one another."

Hebrews 10:24-25 (NIV)

Encouragement is one of the most powerful, strategic, and often overlooked responsibilities in leadership. Many leaders focus on metrics, outcomes, or expectations, while overlooking a simple truth. People perform better when they feel supported. They endure longer when they feel valued. They rise higher when someone believes in their potential. Encouragement is not a soft skill. It is a leadership strength that fuels perseverance, unity, and purpose.

Hebrews 10:24–25 commands believers to spur one another on. This requires intentionality. Leaders must notice effort, affirm progress, and remind others why their work matters.

Encouragement is not merely a positive comment. It is a sacred act of leadership that acknowledges human weariness and speaks life where pressure has drained confidence. It is also a form of presence. Showing up consistently, listening well, and offering honest affirmation reflects a leader who takes responsibility for the emotional and spiritual climate of the team.

This week invites you to explore how God may be calling you to use your leadership voice to strengthen others. You will reflect on your responsibility to encourage, examine the culture you are shaping, and consider how your presence can become a source of strength for the people God has trusted into your care.

Leadership Wisdom for the Christian Leader

Teams do not always need new strategies or tighter expectations to move forward. Sometimes they simply need to be reminded that their work matters and that they are not unnoticed. Workplaces become heavy when people serve under pressure without affirmation. Fatigue grows quietly. Disconnection spreads quickly. Leaders who ignore the emotional climate of their teams eventually see motivation decline, not because people lack skill, but because they lack support.

Hebrews 10:24–25 offers a blueprint for leaders who want to build a healthy culture. Encouragement is not an occasional gesture. It is an ongoing commitment. It is the leader's responsibility to strengthen others, to provide perspective during difficult seasons, and to create spaces where people feel valued. This kind of leadership does more than lift morale. It builds trust. People follow more faithfully when they believe their leader sees them, appreciates them, and is invested in their growth.

Encouragement is a ministry. It turns leaders into carriers of hope. It helps people persevere through challenges that once felt overwhelming. Leaders who consistently encourage create environments where individuals flourish, where teamwork becomes stronger, and where unity replaces isolation. Encouraging leadership reflects the heart of Christ, who never overlooked the weary and never failed to strengthen those entrusted to Him.

Weekly Practice in Faith

This week, take encouragement from a general intention to a deliberate practice. Identify two individuals who may be carrying unseen strain or discouragement. Quietly pray for them. Then speak life into their week by offering sincere and specific encouragement. Mention the strengths you see in them and the impact they are making.

Examine your leadership habits as well. Do your meetings reflect appreciation, or only evaluation? Do you offer feedback that builds, or feedback that only corrects? Choose one practice that centers encouragement in your leadership this week.

Encouragement is an expression of responsibility. It shows others that you take their well-being seriously and that you are committed to nurturing their growth.

Time for Reflection

Encouragement is part of the leader's calling. Hebrews 10:24–25 urges believers to gather with purpose and to strengthen one another with intention. Take time to consider where God may be asking you to step in with encouragement. Who on your team feels unnoticed or worn down? Who may be drifting because no one has spoken belief into their life lately?

Reflect on the weight your words carry. Leaders shape atmospheres. Leaders influence morale. Leaders often determine whether someone feels hopeful or defeated. Ask God to help you notice those who need support and to make your presence a source of comfort, courage, and spiritual strength.

Weekly Prayer

Lord, thank You for entrusting me with the responsibility to strengthen those I lead. Help me notice the weary, support the overlooked, and offer encouragement that restores hope. Shape my words so they lift others up. Shape my presence so it reflects Your grace. Teach me to use my leadership influence wisely, and let my encouragement point people back to You. In Jesus' name, Amen.

WEEK 38

Motivate by Offering Compassion

"If one part suffers, every part suffers with it;

if one part is honored, every part rejoices with it."

1 Corinthians 12:26 (NIV)

Leadership often brings a strong desire to keep people energized, focused, and moving toward shared goals. There are seasons when a team needs vision, enthusiasm, and the steady voice of a leader who calls them forward. Yet there are other seasons when motivation takes a different form. It becomes quieter, more attentive, and rooted in compassion rather than momentum.

People do not leave their lives at the door when they come to work. They bring their burdens with them. When their energy drops or their engagement fades, the cause is rarely laziness. More often, it is a sign of emotional exhaustion, personal struggle, or discouragement that has gone unnoticed. First Corinthians 12:26

reminds us that when one person suffers, everyone feels it. Teams are not collections of isolated performers; they are interconnected human beings. When one person struggles, the leader must feel it too.

Motivation that ignores struggle becomes pressure. Motivation that acknowledges suffering becomes compassion. This week invites you to see your leadership role not only as the one who drives progress, but as the one who notices pain. Before igniting passion, you may need to offer presence. Before expecting renewed effort, you may need to extend understanding. Compassion is often the soil where lasting motivation grows.

Leadership Wisdom for the Christian Leader

There are days when a team appears unmotivated on the surface, yet beneath the quiet meetings and delayed tasks is something far more personal. People carry invisible burdens. These struggles affect the group long before they are spoken aloud. Leaders who pay attention to these moments gain clarity that data alone can never provide.

First Corinthians 12:26 shows us a leadership truth rooted in Christian community. When one person is hurting, the entire group is affected. Healthy leadership recognizes this connection and responds with care. Compassion does not slow progress. It sustains it. Compassionate leaders create an atmosphere where people can be honest without fear of judgment, and where support is offered freely rather than grudgingly.

Emotional intelligence helps leaders see beyond behavior and into the conditions shaping it. A leader who listens well, observes quietly, and responds with humility builds trust that cannot be manufactured. When people feel safe to speak honestly about their struggles, teams strengthen. Workloads can be adjusted, resources can be shared, and solutions can be created collaboratively. Productivity rises, not because pressure increases, but because people feel valued.

This kind of leadership reflects the way Christ cared for those around Him. He noticed the weary before they spoke. He honored the hurting before He gave instruction. Leaders who imitate that posture cultivate cultures where compassion is seen as strength. In such environments, people find the courage to reengage and the motivation to keep moving because they feel understood rather than dismissed.

Weekly Practice in Faith

This week, ask God to help you become more attentive to the emotional climate of those you lead. Choose one or two team members who seem quieter, more fatigued, or less engaged than usual. Schedule intentional moments to check in. Focus on listening rather than problem solving.

Practice motivation by noticing. Ask God to heighten your awareness of subtle signals in conversations or behaviors. Let your presence communicate value more than your expectations communicate urgency. When leaders make space for compassion, they often unlock the very motivation they were hoping to inspire.

Time for Reflection

Leadership places you in a position where the burdens of others affect you, whether you recognize it or not. First Corinthians 12:26 calls you to acknowledge this connection and respond to it with care. Before considering productivity, goals, or timelines, think about the people behind the work. Who may be suffering quietly? Who may be carrying a load that others cannot see?

Reflect on the emotional condition of your team. Consider how compassion might shape your next step. Ask God to help you discern whether the moment calls for encouragement, patience, or simply a listening ear. Motivation becomes stronger when people know their leader is present with them, not just expecting from them.

Weekly Prayer

Lord, help me see the needs of those You have entrusted to my care. Give me a compassionate heart and the awareness to notice when someone is hurting. Teach me to motivate through understanding and to lead with a spirit that reflects Your gentleness. Use my presence to bring comfort and my words to bring hope. In Jesus' name, Amen.

WEEK 39

A Leader's Source of Motivation

"For we live by faith, not by sight."

2 Corinthians 5-7 (NIV)

There will be seasons in leadership when progress is slow, outcomes are uncertain, and every effort feels heavier than the last. These moments reveal something important. Leaders need motivation too. Fatigue, discouragement, or unmet expectations can drain a leader's confidence and influence. Yet Scripture directs our eyes to a deeper truth. Real motivation does not come from visible results. It comes from faith.

Second Corinthians 5:7 is more than a spiritual reminder. It is a leadership anchor. To live by faith rather than sight means choosing to serve from conviction rather than convenience. It means showing up when results lag, making wise decisions even when clarity is thin, and trusting that God is working in ways you cannot yet see. A leader who serves from faith becomes a steady presence for others. Faith fuels consistency. It strengthens integrity. It gives people hope.

This week invites you to reflect on what truly drives your leadership. Are you motivated by recognition or certainty, or by a deep trust in the God who sees what you cannot? When a leader serves from faith, their actions inspire others to endure, believe, and keep moving forward.

Leadership Wisdom for the Christian Leader

Some seasons of leadership feel like standing in front of a problem with limited resources and an overwhelming need. Leaders often face shrinking budgets, delayed results, discouraged teams, or complex circumstances that do not add up to success. In these moments, sight can fail you. It points to limitation. Faith points to God's provision.

Second Corinthians 5:7 calls leaders to move beyond what is immediately visible. Faith shaped leadership does not ignore reality. It simply refuses to be ruled by it. Leaders who trust God learn to navigate uncertainty with calm conviction. Their service becomes an act of worship rather than a response to outcomes. They continue to serve faithfully, steward wisely, and encourage consistently because they believe God can work in ways that stretch far beyond human calculation.

Faith requires movement. Leaders who serve by faith take steps guided by trust, not pressure. They lead with patience when others rush ahead. They persevere with integrity when shortcuts appear tempting. They motivate teams by reminding them that unseen progress is still progress. God multiplies what is offered to Him with trust and humility. Leaders anchored in faith help their teams envision a future shaped not by fear, but by God's steady hand.

Weekly Practice in Faith

This week, reflect on how faith shapes your service. Identify one area where you have been hesitant to act because you cannot yet see the outcome. Bring that specific situation to God in prayer. Ask Him to strengthen your trust, renew your motivation, and guide your steps.

Choose one act of service to complete this week without expecting recognition or immediate results. Serve someone quietly and intentionally. Let this be a discipline that redirects your focus from what is seen to what is eternal.

Time for Reflection

Faith calls leaders to move even when the results are not visible. It strengthens the resolve to serve consistently, without needing applause or immediate success. Leadership can feel lonely in seasons where progress is gradual or hidden, yet God uses these moments to form deeper strength: patience, humility, and spiritual resilience.

Think back to a moment when slow results challenged your motivation. Did you try to push forward in your own strength, or did you pause long enough to realign with God's perspective? Faith reorients your service. It reminds you that leadership is an offering, not a performance.

Ask God to help you see where He is already at work. Ask Him for the courage to keep serving, even when progress is quiet. Leadership that is grounded in faith leaves a lasting impact because it points people to a God who never stops working, even when the path ahead is hidden.

Weekly Prayer

Lord, thank You for being faithful even when I cannot see what lies ahead. Strengthen my motivation in seasons of slow progress. Teach me to serve with faith filled consistency and trust You with the results. Shape my leadership so that it reflects Your character and encourages others to hope in You. In Jesus' name, Amen.

WEEK 40

Recognition and Affirmation Goes a Long Way

"Gracious words are a honeycomb,

sweet to the soul and healing to the bones.."

Proverbs 16:24 (NIV)

Leadership is not only about direction and decision making. At its core, leadership is about people. People carry burdens you cannot see. They invest effort you may never know. Even the strongest, most resilient individuals need to hear that their work matters.

Think back to a moment when your effort went unnoticed. You were not seeking applause, but a simple acknowledgment would have strengthened your spirit. Proverbs 16:24 reminds us that gracious words carry healing power. Like honey that restores strength, sincere affirmation nourishes the heart and brings life into weary places.

Many leaders underestimate the weight of recognition. Encouragement does not weaken standards. It strengthens the commitment behind them. A timely word can shift a discouraged teammate toward renewed resolve. It can soften tension, mend relationships, and build trust. Encouragement is not flattery. It is the intentional choice to see the good, to honor effort, and to affirm the image of God in others.

This week invites you to reflect on your responsibility to speak life. As a leader, your words carry influence. They can drain or restore. They can silence or strengthen. When your leadership is marked by gracious affirmation, you join God in the work of building others up.

Leadership Wisdom for the Christian Leader

Words shape the emotional climate of every team. They can create stability or anxiety, hope or hesitation. Leaders often focus on strategies, processes, or performance indicators, but God uses something far simpler to transform the human heart. A sincere, well timed word of affirmation can rekindle motivation where exhaustion has taken hold.

Proverbs 16:24 offers a powerful reminder. Gracious words bring sweetness and healing. They restore what stress and disappointment have worn down. Leaders who choose gracious speech communicate value and dignity. They remind their teams that their work is meaningful and that their contributions serve a purpose beyond the task itself.

This kind of leadership creates trust. When people feel seen and appreciated, they work with deeper engagement. Gracious words encourage perseverance because they speak to the person, not just their performance. Over time, cultures shaped by affirmation become stronger, healthier, and more united. People begin to lift one another, encourage one another, and take ownership of the atmosphere they help create.

When leaders choose graciousness in their speech, they reflect the character of Christ who consistently uplifted, strengthened, and restored. Encouragement is more than a technique. It is an act of stewardship and a powerful form of spiritual leadership.

Weekly Practice in Faith

This week, practice the discipline of intentional affirmation. Identify three people in your sphere of influence who receive little recognition. Offer them specific, meaningful encouragement. It may be a handwritten note, a spoken word, or a message of gratitude.

Affirm effort, not just outcomes. Celebrate progress, not only results. Recognize quiet acts of faithfulness that often go unseen.

As you practice this, notice how it shapes your own spirit. Affirmation often blesses the giver as much as the receiver.

Time for Reflection

Take a quiet moment to consider the power your words held this week. Were they life giving or draining? Did you affirm more than you corrected? Scripture reminds us that gracious words heal. They strengthen weary hearts and restore hope where discouragement lingers.

Think of someone under your leadership who may be carrying unseen burdens. Ask God to give you insight into their needs and the courage to speak with intentional grace. Leadership becomes transformative when your words help others stand taller than they did before.

Weekly Prayer

Lord, thank You for the healing power of gracious words. Help me to lead with encouragement that reflects Your love and truth. Teach me to recognize the efforts of those around me and to affirm them with sincerity. May my words bring strength, healing, and renewed purpose to those I serve. In Jesus' name, Amen.

Leadership and the Cross
THE
FEAR OF TAKING THE LEAD

> **Weeks 41 - 45**
>
> Leadership often brings hidden fear: *What will it cost to step up?* Many hesitate; not because they lack ability, but because they fear judgment, rejection, or falling short. The pressure to be perfect or please everyone can quietly hold leaders back.
>
> This theme explores the struggles beneath leadership reluctance: fear of scrutiny, failure, and disappointing others. But more importantly, it points to a deeper truth; God doesn't call us to lead with perfection, but with obedience. You'll be reminded that courage in leadership isn't about having all the answers, but trusting the One who does.

WEEK 41

The Fear of Scrutiny and Criticism

"Do not be afraid of them, for I am with you and will rescue you."
Jeremiah 1:8 (NIV)

Leadership is not only about talent or strategy. It is about courage. Leaders are called to step forward, speak truth, make decisions, and shoulder responsibility. These actions naturally invite observation. They attract opinions, assumptions, and at times unfair criticism. Many gifted leaders never rise to their potential because the fear of what others perceive becomes louder than their calling.

The spotlight of leadership exposes strengths and weaknesses. A bold decision may be questioned. A necessary change may be misunderstood. A step of initiative may be misinterpreted. Over time, hesitation sets in. Leaders begin to doubt themselves, delay action, or choose silence to avoid scrutiny.

Yet God does not call the fearless. He calls the willing. When Jeremiah received his assignment, he immediately pulled back. He questioned his readiness, his voice, and his credibility. God did not respond with a list of strengths or a leadership plan. He offered His presence. "Do not be afraid of them, for I am with you." For every leader who shrinks under the weight of criticism or feels exposed in leadership, that promise still stands.

Jeremiah's calling reveals a truth every leader must embrace. God's presence is the foundation for courage. Stepping forward is not reckless. It is an act of trust. Leaders who sacrifice their comfort and choose obedience discover strength that does not depend on public approval. When fear whispers "hold back," God reminds you to step forward with confidence rooted in Him.

Leadership Wisdom for the Christian Leader

Leadership often places people in positions where their actions, ideas, and motives become visible before they feel prepared. Even seasoned leaders wrestle with the quiet fear of being evaluated, misjudged, or criticized. Expectations rise. Opinions multiply. The pressure can feel overwhelming.

Jeremiah 1:8 offers a stabilizing truth. Leaders do not stand alone in moments of scrutiny. God's presence does not vanish when the meeting grows tense, the questions grow sharp, or the pressure becomes personal. He stands with those who step into difficult assignments, providing clarity when their words are challenged and strength when their courage feels thin.

Courage that is rooted in God does not erase fear. It steadies the heart. Leaders who walk into scrutiny with confidence in God's presence speak with greater clarity, react with more humility, and lead with composure even when the environment feels intimidating. Their confidence is not built on applause but on obedience. Over time, this kind of courage shapes a leader who is resilient, calm under pressure, and trustworthy.

When leaders face criticism with dignity rather than defensiveness, they inspire those around them. Their teams learn that courage is not loud. It is steady. It is anchored. It is faithful. Leaders who lean into God's presence model a kind of strength that invites others to rise with them. They cultivate cultures where people step forward without fear, serve boldly, and lead with confidence grounded in something far greater than human opinion.

Weekly Practice in Faith

This week, identify one area where fear of criticism has caused you to hesitate. It may involve speaking up, offering a new idea, addressing a difficult issue, or making a decision that others might question.

Bring that situation before God in prayer. Read Jeremiah 1:8 slowly and let its promise settle into your spirit. Commit to taking one faithful step forward. Courage grows through action, and God honors leaders who move in faith even when uncertainty lingers.

Time for Reflection

Leadership naturally exposes you to the opinions of others. Scrutiny can feel heavy, especially when you doubt your capacity or fear being misunderstood. Jeremiah felt the same tension, yet God reminded him that obedience mattered more than public approval.

Reflect on a moment when fear caused you to pull back from a necessary action. Consider what might have changed if you had believed more deeply that God stood beside you in that moment. His presence is not symbolic. It is active, protective, and empowering. Ask Him to help you see leadership moments not as opportunities to be judged but as invitations to trust Him more deeply.

Weekly Prayer

Lord, I confess the times I have hesitated to lead because of fear, criticism, or doubt. Thank You for reminding me that Your presence is stronger than any opinion spoken against me. Strengthen my heart and steady my spirit. Give me the courage to lead boldly, with humility and faith. Help me reflect Your character more than I protect my own comfort. In Jesus' name, Amen.

WEEK 42

The Fear of Having to be Perfect

"My grace is sufficient for you,
for my power is made perfect in weakness."
2 Corinthians 12:9 (NIV)

Perfectionism hides well in leadership. It often looks like excellence, preparation, or high standards. But underneath, it is usually fear. Fear of disappointing people. Fear of being misunderstood. Fear of appearing inadequate. Many leaders quietly measure their worth by flawless performance, believing that a single mistake reflects a flaw in who they are.

But leadership is not sustained by perfection. It is sustained by grace. Second Corinthians 12:9 reminds us that God's strength shines most clearly in our limitations. Leaders who rest in grace begin to lead from identity rather than insecurity. You do not earn your worth through polished execution. Your value comes from who you are in Christ, not from what you accomplish.

This week, you are invited to release the pressure that perfectionism brings. Leadership rooted in grace frees both you and those you lead. It shifts the focus from proving yourself to trusting the God who empowers you.

Leadership Wisdom for the Christian Leader

Leadership environments often reward flawless performance. Teams expect answers. Stakeholders expect results. When expectations rise, leaders sometimes slip into a mindset where mistakes feel unacceptable. Instead of admitting struggle, they hide it. They work harder, rehearse longer, and carry the silent pressure to appear unshakable. But hidden strain does not disappear. It grows until something gives.

This pattern is especially dangerous for Christian leaders because it slowly erodes the awareness of grace. Leadership becomes a burden to manage rather than a calling to serve. Over time, anxiety replaces peace. Pressure replaces presence. Joy fades under the weight of self-imposed standards.

Second Corinthians 12:9 offers a radically different way to lead. God tells us His power is made perfect in weakness. This truth dismantles the lie that leadership requires flawlessness. Weakness does not disqualify you. It becomes the doorway where God's strength can be most clearly seen. Leaders who lean into this truth stop trying to carry what only God can hold. They lead with more honesty, more humility, and more dependence on God's sustaining grace.

When a leader stops performing and starts leading from grace, the culture around them shifts. People feel safer to ask questions, admit mistakes, and pursue growth instead of perfection. Stress decreases and collaboration increases. Excellence improves, not because pressure intensifies, but because the environment becomes healthier. Leaders who model grace create teams where people can be human and still strive for meaningful outcomes. In such places, God's power fills the gaps, steadies the pace, and builds confidence that is rooted in Him alone.

Weekly Practice in Faith

This week, resist the urge to perfect every detail. Choose one specific area where you tend to overthink or overwork due to fear of missing something. Invite God into that place. Say, "Lord, Your grace is sufficient. Lead me in this."

Release the need to impress. Lead with presence rather than performance.

Also reflect on whether your perfectionism is placing pressure on others. Consider how modeling grace might relieve unnecessary tension within your team or family. Leadership shaped by grace gives people permission to breathe.

Time for Reflection

Where in your leadership are you trying to prove yourself? Consider the quiet pressure you carry to be flawless: the need to impress, the fear of being misunderstood, or the hesitation to admit limits. These pressures often reveal misplaced trust. Perfectionism grows where fear has replaced faith.

Second Corinthians 12:9 reminds you that God does not require perfection. He calls you to obedience, faithfulness, and trust. God's power rests on you most fully when you stop performing and start surrendering.

Reflect on how your authenticity might encourage others. Sometimes the most powerful leadership moment comes through admitting weakness and allowing God's strength to be seen through you.

Weekly Prayer

Father, I confess the times I have tried to earn worth through performance. I carry expectations and pressure that You never asked me to hold. Teach me to lead from grace, not fear. Help me release the burden of perfection and rest in Your sufficiency. Let Your strength shine where I feel weak. Shape my leadership with courage, honesty, and trust. In Jesus' name, Amen.

WEEK 43

The Fear of Disappointing Others

"Cast your cares on the Lord and he will sustain you;

he will never let the righteous be shaken."

Psalm 55:22 (NIV)

Herbert Bayard Swope, a Pulitzer Prize-winning journalist, is quoted as saying, *"I can't give you a sure-fire formula for success, but I can give you a formula for failure: try to please everybody all the time."*

Leaders know this truth well. Leadership is not only about guiding tasks or teams. It often involves carrying the hopes, expectations, and emotional weight of the people you serve. That desire to care well can slowly transform into a paralyzing fear of letting others down. Leaders begin to think their worth is tied to how consistently they meet everyone's expectations or avoid disappointing anyone who depends on them.

This fear distorts leadership. It leads to over-functioning, micromanagement, constant apologizing, or avoiding conflict. It convinces leaders that they must hold every burden together in their own strength. But Scripture gives a much different instruction. Psalm 55:22 does not tell you to carry the weight better. It tells you to release it. God invites you to cast your cares on Him and promises to sustain you. You were never designed to carry the emotional load of leadership alone.

This week invites you to examine where the responsibility to lead has subtly shifted into an unhealthy pressure to please. God calls leaders to responsibility, not perfection. To faithfulness, not people-pleasing. The same God who sustains creation sustains leaders too.

Leadership Wisdom for the Christian Leader

There is a quiet pressure felt most deeply by leaders with compassionate hearts. It is not the stress of deadlines or logistics. It is the internal fear of disappointing someone who has placed trust in you. Leaders who care deeply often carry the heaviest emotional burden. They step in quickly, take on too much, and try to shield everyone from hardship. They mistake caring for controlling and assume God expects them to keep everyone happy.

Psalm 55:22 speaks directly to this fear. God does not ask leaders to carry every expectation. He asks them to cast their cares on Him. Leadership becomes distorted when the fear of disappointing others becomes greater than the desire to obey God. When leaders release that fear to the Lord, they become healthier, steadier, and more authentic. Responsibility remains, but pressure lifts. Leaders stop absorbing every emotion and start guiding teams with honesty, clarity, and shared ownership.

When leaders trust God with what they cannot control, their presence becomes calmer and their leadership more grounded. The fear of disappointing others loosens its grip because the leader's worth is no longer tied to flawless outcomes. Teams flourish under leaders whose confidence rests in God rather than in meeting every expectation. Healthy leadership grows from surrender, not perfection.

Weekly Practice in Faith

Identify one situation you have been carrying that does not fully belong to you. It may be a team conflict, a strained relationship, or pressure to meet someone's expectation. Write it down.

Each morning this week, take five slow minutes to intentionally cast that care on the Lord. Say aloud, "This burden is not mine alone." Ask God to give you wisdom for what is yours to handle and courage to release what is not.

Remember that love does not require over-functioning. Leadership does not require pleasing everyone. Faithfulness does not require carrying every burden.

Time for Reflection

Take a quiet moment to consider the emotional load you have been shouldering. Has responsibility slowly turned into pressure? Have you equated disappointment with failure? Have you assumed that if you let go, everything will fall apart?

Psalm 55:22 offers a different vision. God sustains you. God upholds the people you lead. God carries what you cannot. Reflect on what it would look like to truly cast your leadership burdens onto the Lord. Ask Him to reveal where obedience ends and personal control begins. Invite His strength into the places where yours has worn thin.

Weekly Prayer

Lord, I confess that I often try to carry what You never asked me to hold. I care for those I lead, yet sometimes that care becomes fear, pressure, and exhaustion. Teach me to lead with responsibility without taking on the weight of perfection. Help me to cast my burdens on You daily, trusting that You sustain me and the people I serve. Quiet my fear of disappointing others and root my confidence in You alone. Amen.

WEEK 44

The Fear of Rejection

"So do not fear, for I am with you; do not be dismayed, for I am your God. I will strengthen you and help you; I will uphold you with my righteous right hand."

Isaiah 41:10 (NIV)

Rejection leaves a lasting mark. Leaders feel this deeply, not through loud criticism alone, but often through silence, withdrawal, or the absence of support. You pour yourself into a project or decision and watch it go unnoticed or dismissed. The next time, you hesitate. You pull back. You play it safe. Vulnerability begins to feel dangerous, so you lock parts of your leadership behind caution.

This fear hides beneath polished professionalism. Leaders call it strategy or emotional maturity, yet often it is self-protection. To avoid rejection, leaders stop sharing bold ideas, delay important decisions, and avoid hard conversations. Leadership becomes a performance instead of a calling. But God never requested that kind of leadership. He calls His people to obedience, not approval. He calls leaders to show up fully, with courage shaped by His presence, not the acceptance of others.

Jesus understands the pain of rejection more than anyone. He was misunderstood, dismissed, betrayed, and abandoned. Yet His obedience never wavered. His identity was not anchored in human approval but in the assurance of His Father's presence. Isaiah 41:10 reminds Christian leaders that rejection from people does not equal abandonment from God. He holds you. He strengthens you. He sustains you when your efforts are dismissed or your voice is overlooked.

This week, you will confront how deeply the fear of rejection affects your leadership and reflect on what it means to obey God even when approval is not guaranteed.

Leadership Wisdom for the Christian Leader

Few fears shape leadership more quietly than the fear of being rejected. Many leaders operate in cultures where psychological safety is low and trust is fragile. When ideas are mocked, belittled, or ignored, leaders learn to hold back. They begin managing emotions rather than stewarding their call. This fear rarely presents itself openly. It shows up in hesitation, silence, and self-editing. Over time, leaders become spectators rather than shepherds.

Isaiah 41:10 speaks with strength into this hidden tension. God tells His people not to fear because He is present, strengthening and upholding them. Leadership grounded in this truth looks different. The leader's confidence no longer depends on applause or agreement. Their courage does not rise and fall with the responses of peers. Their identity rests in the steady presence of God.

Leaders who confront the fear of rejection become more resilient. They speak truth with clarity and humility. They stop avoiding hard conversations and begin leading with conviction. Their teams experience stability because the leader is no longer shaped by who approves or disapproves. Leadership becomes an act of obedience to God rather than a negotiation for acceptance. This shift brings freedom. It strengthens the leader. It strengthens the culture. It strengthens the mission.

Weekly Practice in Faith

Think about moments when the fear of rejection influenced your leadership decisions. Identify two specific situations this week where you felt a tension between doing what is right and doing what is popular. Write them down.

Pray over each situation and ask God to help you respond with obedience rather than hesitation. Choose one act of leadership you will carry out this week with courage and clarity. It might be a necessary conversation, a decision you have been avoiding, or a truth you need to speak.

Read Isaiah 41:10 before you take that step. Allow God's promise of presence and strength to shape your response.

Time for Reflection

Consider with this question: Who are you leading for? Approval or obedience? Popularity or purpose?
Let this settle in your spirit.

Isaiah 41:10 invites you to lead from a place of confidence rooted in God's presence. Reflect on how often you adjust your leadership for the sake of acceptance. Pray for a heart that values God's voice above public response. Ask Him to help you release the fear of rejection so you can lead with authenticity, strength, and peace.

Weekly Prayer

Father, You know the desire in my heart to be accepted and understood. You also know how often that desire influences my decisions. Forgive me for the times I have led from fear rather than from faith. Strengthen me with Your presence when I feel uncertain. Remind me that Your approval matters more than the opinions of others. Help me lead with courage, clarity, and obedience. Let Your voice be louder than my fear of rejection. In Jesus' name, Amen.

WEEK 45

Understand God's Definition of Success

"Well done, good and faithful servant!
You have been faithful with a few things;
I will put you in charge of many things."

Matthew 25:21 (NIV)

In leadership, success is often measured by clear metrics: growth, profit, performance, approval. Goals are tracked, results are analyzed, and evaluations hinge on whether the outcome matched the expectations. But what happens when we give our best, stay faithful, and things still don't go as planned? The world will call this falling short of expectations or even failure.

Leaders frequently carry the weight of results on their shoulders. We convince ourselves that productivity is the same as impact, and that visible wins are the only proof of good leadership. But

Scripture paints a different picture. Matthew 25:21 reminds us that God's commendation does not begin with "Well done, successful leader." It begins with "Well done, good and faithful servant." In God's Kingdom, success is not defined by how much we accomplish, but by how faithfully we steward what He entrusts to us.

Leadership Wisdom for the Christian Leader

Leaders often carry silent pressure to produce outcomes that validate their worth. They study metrics, compare their progress to others, and feel discouraged when growth slows or influence seems small. Yet Scripture offers a different measure. God never asked leaders to manufacture success. He asked them to steward what He placed in their hands with faithfulness.

Matthew 25:21 reminds leaders that God's highest praise is reserved for those who remain faithful in the quiet, consistent work that others may overlook. Faithfulness is not passive. It is a steady commitment to serve with excellence even when progress is invisible, recognition is limited, and impact seems small. God sees every sacrifice, every unseen hour, and every act of obedience that no one else notices.

When leaders redefine success through faithfulness, their influence grows deeper rather than broader. They begin investing in people rather than chasing prestige. They value transformation more than visibility. This kind of leadership leaves a legacy that numbers cannot capture. God often multiplies the work of a leader whose life is rooted in faith, humility, and obedience. True Kingdom success is not measured by how high you climb but by how well you serve.

Weekly Practice in Faith

This week, take time to evaluate how you measure success in your leadership and daily life. Ask yourself whether your sense of accomplishment is tied to outcomes or to obedience. Begin each morning with a simple prayer: "Lord, help me be faithful today."

Choose one small act of service each day that reflects the love of Christ. It may not move a chart or earn applause, but it will shape your heart. At the end of the week, measure success by faithfulness rather than productivity. Ask God to help you view your leadership through His eyes, not the eyes of others.

Time for Reflection

Reflect on the areas where you feel pressure to perform. Are those pressures rooted in God's expectations or in your own? Think about a moment when you served well but struggled to see results. How might God have been working behind the scenes in ways you could not see. Success in God's Kingdom is not about outcomes. It is about the steady obedience of a servant who trusts that God sees, God knows, and God multiplies what is offered to Him.

Weekly Prayer

Lord, thank You for redefining success in a way that brings peace instead of pressure. Teach me to value faithfulness over recognition and obedience over achievement. Help me release the need to prove myself and to lead from a place of trust rather than striving. Shape my heart to reflect Your priorities and let my leadership bring honor to You. May my service point others to Your faithfulness. In Jesus' name, Amen.

Leadership and the Cross

THE ETHICAL LEADER

Weeks 46 - 50

Ethical leadership is about more than doing good things; it's about becoming the kind of person God can trust with influence. In a culture that often celebrates shortcuts, ego, or results at any cost, Christian leaders are called to something deeper. True leadership starts with integrity and is sustained by accountability, clarity, and courage. Each decision becomes a reflection of the One we serve, not just a strategy for getting ahead. This theme explores what it means to lead with conviction: keeping integrity at your core, accepting responsibility, standing on God's standards, protecting those in your care, and embracing the real cost of doing what is right. When ethics lead, trust follows and so does lasting impact.

WEEK 46

The Core of any Leader is their Integrity

"Whoever walks in integrity walks securely,

but whoever takes crooked paths will be found out."

Proverbs 10:9 (NIV)

Ethics may shape policies, but integrity shapes people. It is the foundation beneath every leader's influence. Without integrity, no combination of charisma, vision, or success can create lasting trust. Leaders may impress others for a season, but if their character is compromised, their leadership eventually collapses. Proverbs 10:9 makes the promise clear. Those who walk in integrity walk securely. This security does not guarantee freedom from hardship, but it does promise God's favor on those who remain faithful and upright.

The temptation to compromise rarely arrives dramatically. It creeps in through small moments of convenience. It whispers through exaggerating progress, bending numbers, masking failure, or choosing image over honesty. These choices often feel minor, but each one chips away at a leader's credibility. Integrity chooses transparency when hiding would be easier. It chooses honesty when self-preservation feels safer. It chooses consistency when applause is absent. Integrity keeps a leader's inner world aligned with their words, values, and commitments.

As you enter this theme on ethics, remember that integrity is not perfection. It is alignment. It is living in such a way that your character is the same in private as it is in public. Leaders who walk in integrity lead with calm confidence because their conscience is clear and their path is straight. This week invites you to examine whether integrity is truly the center of your leadership and whether your choices reflect a heart anchored in Christ.

Leadership Wisdom for the Christian Leader

Leadership often places people in situations where they see the truth long before others do. A small pattern emerges. A metric shifts. A concern surfaces. In those moments, leaders face a defining choice. They can protect their image, stay silent, or hope problems disappear. Or they can tell the truth while the cost is still small. Integrity rarely shouts. It whispers. Yet it is that whisper that determines the direction of the leader and the stability of the organization.

Proverbs 10:9 reminds us that integrity builds a secure path. This is not about safety or popularity. It is about walking before God with a heart that refuses to twist the truth. Integrity means choosing what is right when no one sees it. It means practicing accountability even when no one demands it. It means letting truth guide your steps instead of convenience or pressure. Leaders who choose integrity gain trust because their lives stand on solid ground. There is nothing hidden to uncover. Nothing crooked to straighten. Nothing to fear in the light.

When integrity becomes the core of leadership, cultures change. Teams feel safe. Trust grows. People speak honestly. Problems surface sooner. Solutions come faster. Teams no longer hide mistakes, because their leader has shown that truth is always welcomed, even when it is difficult. A leader who walks in integrity creates an environment strong enough to withstand pressure because its foundation is truth. God honors the leader who chooses the straight path, even when it is the hardest one to take.

Weekly Practice in Faith

Return to Proverbs 10:9 throughout the week and ask God to reveal any area where your path has begun to drift. Identify one place where integrity needs strengthening, whether in communication, accountability, or decision making. Then make one intentional choice that reflects a commitment to walk securely with God. Choose integrity in a place where it will cost you something, even if no one will ever know. God sees. God strengthens. God honors the upright.

Time for Reflection

Integrity is not about flawless leadership. It is about consistent alignment between what you believe and how you behave. The security described in Proverbs 10:9 comes from a clear conscience and a steady heart. When leaders choose honesty over convenience and truth over image, they build trust that cannot be shaken by pressure or performance.

Reflect on the choices before you this week. Are there areas where shortcuts or silence are tempting? Are you protecting your image instead of confronting reality? Ask God to strengthen your resolve to walk uprightly even when the cost is high. Lasting peace comes when your leadership aligns fully with His truth.

Weekly Prayer

Lord, thank You for being a God of truth. Shape my heart to walk in integrity even when the path is difficult. Give me the strength to resist shortcuts and compromises that diminish my witness. Help my words, decisions, and actions reflect the character of Christ so that those I lead may find security in my example. Keep me steady and faithful, trusting You to honor the upright path. Amen.

WEEK 47

All Leaders are Accountable; All Christians are Accountable

"So then, each of us will give an account of ourselves to God."

Romans 14:12 (NIV

In every sphere of life, one truth remains constant: no one leads without being accountable to someone or something. This is a universal principle that transcends position, industry, or status. Leaders are accountable for their decisions, and Christians are accountable for their lives before God. Whether you oversee a team, a ministry, a household, or your own conduct, accountability is not optional. It is built into the very fabric of leadership and faith.

Romans 14:12 draws a direct line between earthly responsibility and eternal accountability. "Each of us will give an account of ourselves to God." Leadership roles may differ, and life circumstances may vary, but this truth remains the same for all. Just as a leader must answer for what has been entrusted to them, every believer must answer to God for how they stewarded their influence, motives, and choices.

Integrity forms the foundation. Accountability forms the structure. One cannot exist securely without the other. And while accountability may feel uncomfortable, restrictive, or inconvenient in the moment, it is a safeguard that protects both leaders and those they serve. It ensures that decisions are not made carelessly, that character guides conduct, and that responsibility replaces complacency.

This week, you are invited to embrace accountability not as punishment, but as a gift. It is the discipline that strengthens character, the guardrail that preserves integrity, and the spiritual reminder that your leadership and your faith are lived before the eyes of God.

Leadership Wisdom for the Christian Leader

Leadership becomes dangerous when accountability disappears. Without it, even strong leaders can drift into isolated decision making, lose perspective, and forget how their choices affect others. Some resist accountability because it invites honest questions. Others fear it because it forces them to confront uncomfortable truths. But the absence of accountability is not freedom. It is the slow erosion of character and trust.

Romans 14:12 reminds leaders that accountability is not just horizontal, it is vertical. Authority is always tied to stewardship. Influence is always tied to responsibility. And every decision ultimately stands before God, who sees motives as clearly as actions. This truth does not intimidate a healthy leader; it anchors them. It keeps pride from taking root and prevents isolation from shaping their judgment.

Accountable leaders are not weakened by transparency. They are strengthened by it. Their willingness to be open signals that they have nothing to hide and everything to protect. Teams learn that honesty is safe, correction is welcome, and shared responsibility is expected. Leaders who embrace accountability create cultures where people can speak up, own mistakes, and grow without fear. Leadership becomes healthier because it is grounded in truth rather than image.

In the long run, accountability preserves integrity, strengthens influence, and honors God. Leaders who live by this principle stand on solid ground because they lead with a clear conscience and an open heart. Accountability does not diminish authority. It purifies it.

Weekly Practice in Faith

This week, approach leadership with a renewed awareness that every decision, word, and action ultimately answers to God. Accountability is not about fear; it is about stewardship.

Begin each day with a simple prayer:
"Lord, align my motives with Your will. Keep my leadership honest and my heart accountable to You."

Then choose one specific area to open to greater accountability. That could look like:

- asking for honest feedback from someone you trust
- inviting a mentor to review a current decision
- owning a mistake rather than explaining it away
- bringing clarity to something you allowed to remain vague
- correcting an action or attitude you've justified for too long

Accountability strengthens humility and builds credibility. Practicing it will deepen your character and strengthen your leadership.

Time for Reflection

Leadership carries weight not only in the eyes of others but before God Himself. Romans 14:12 reminds us that influence is sacred and that every leader will give account for how they stewarded it. Accountability is not about control; it is about character.

Take a few moments to reflect on how you respond to correction, feedback, or oversight. Do you welcome accountability, or do you avoid it? Are there areas where pride keeps you from inviting perspective? Are there decisions you've made alone that should have been shared?

Ask God to reveal the places where accountability can bring freedom, clarity, and growth. Leadership grounded in truth sets you, your team, and your mission on a secure path.

Weekly Prayer

Lord, I acknowledge that I am accountable to You in all things. Give me humility to receive feedback, courage to correct what needs to be addressed, and wisdom to lead with integrity. Help me to steward the influence You've entrusted to me with honesty and care. May my leadership reflect a heart that values accountability as a gift, not a burden. Strengthen me to honor You in every decision. Amen.

WEEK 48

Leaders Should Begin by Following God's Standards

"Peter and the other apostles replied:
'We must obey God rather than human beings!'"
Acts 5:29 (NIV)

Ethical leadership begins with understanding that every leader is accountable to a higher authority. The world offers shifting standards built on popularity, profit, or perception. Scripture offers a different foundation. Acts 5:29 captures this tension clearly. When the apostles were pressured to compromise, their response was unwavering: obedience to God mattered more than approval from people.

Every leader will face defining moments where values are tested. Do you conform to expectations for the sake of convenience, or do you stand firm in what you know is true? Obedience is not a passive act. It requires courage, conviction, and clarity of purpose. Ethical leadership rooted in obedience is steady because it begins with the question, "What honors God?" not, "What pleases people?"

This week invites you to examine the standards shaping your leadership decisions. Are you fueled by temporary approval or guided by eternal truth? Leaders who choose God's standards build credibility, trust, and strength that cannot be shaken.

Leadership Wisdom for the Christian Leader

Leadership becomes spiritually significant when pressure invites compromise. Deadlines tighten, stakeholders demand results, and the temptation grows to prioritize outcomes over obedience. These crossroads reveal more than decision making ability. They reveal the moral and spiritual framework of a leader.

Acts 5:29 provides a steady compass for these moments. The apostles understood that obedience to God would cost them comfort, approval, and potentially their lives. Yet their loyalty to God's truth anchored them. This same principle applies to leaders today. Leading by God's standards means refusing shortcuts that violate integrity, protecting the vulnerable even when it is inconvenient, and making decisions rooted in righteousness rather than reputation.

When leaders choose obedience over the shifting approval of others, trust grows. Culture strengthens. Teams learn that integrity is not negotiable and that truth shapes decisions more than fear. Leaders anchored in God's standards become stabilizing forces in uncertain environments. Their character sets a tone that influences not only what is done, but how it is done. In God's Kingdom, obedience is success, and faithfulness becomes the testimony that outlasts every temporary sacrifice.

Weekly Practice in Faith

This week, be intentional about recognizing moments when you feel pressured to compromise. Pause before making decisions and ask a single guiding question: "Does this honor God?"

Invite the Holy Spirit to search your motives and expose any places where people pleasing, pride, or convenience may be influencing your choices. If there is a decision you regret, bring it before God. Realign your actions with His truth and trust that obedience always leads to steady footing.

Obedience is a discipline. Practice it in small decisions, and you will stand firm in the large ones.

Time for Reflection

Acts 5:29 challenges every leader to evaluate whose voice carries the most weight in their decision making. The apostles faced intense pressure to remain silent, yet they chose conviction over compromise.

Sit quietly with this thought: Where in your leadership has the desire for approval overshadowed obedience to God? Consider times when you felt tension between what was right and what was easy. Reflect on how choosing God's standards might have changed your posture, your words, or your choices.

Ask God for discernment to recognize future crossroads and strength to choose integrity every time.

Weekly Prayer

Lord, help me to lead with obedience to Your Word above all else. Give me courage when compromise appears easier and strength when pressure rises. Shape my character so that integrity becomes my foundation and faithfulness my priority. Let my leadership reflect Your truth in every decision I make. Amen.

WEEK 49

Ethical Leaders Protect Others

"He has shown you, O mortal, what is good.

And what does the Lord require of you?

To act justly and to love mercy

and to walk humbly with your God."

Micah 6:8 (NIV)

Leadership is never about self advancement. Godly leadership calls for something deeper: to act with justice, extend mercy, and walk humbly with God. These qualities are not optional. They shape the ethical backbone of a leader's life. Every decision you make is like a pebble dropped into a still pond. The ripples will touch lives, influence culture, and either protect or harm the people entrusted to your care.

Micah 6:8 offers one of the clearest summaries of biblical ethics. Do what is right. Lead with compassion. Walk humbly in step with God. Leaders who embrace these principles understand that ethical decisions are not just about organizational outcomes. They are about people. Integrity, fairness, and mercy protect the vulnerable, uphold dignity, and reflect the heart of God.

This week, as you consider what it means to live ethically, remember that true leadership protects. It safeguards those under your influence rather than sacrificing them for convenience or personal success. It builds environments of trust where people know they are valued and safe.

Leadership Wisdom for the Christian Leader

The truest measure of a leader is revealed when someone must step between people and harm. Ethical leadership shows itself most clearly when pressure rises, systems falter, or others are overlooked. Protecting people is not weakness. It is strength anchored in conviction, guided by compassion, and shaped by humility. True protection reflects a leader who sees people as image bearers of God, not as resources to be used or obstacles to be moved. It requires courage to resist the temptation to look away, minimize concerns, or preserve personal comfort when others are at risk.

Micah 6:8 gives leaders a threefold mandate. *Acting justly* means refusing to overlook injustice or ignore decisions that harm people, even in subtle ways. *Loving mercy* means responding with compassion to both the vulnerable and the pressured. *Walking humbly* means relying on God's wisdom rather than pride, and speaking truth even when the truth costs something. Leaders who protect others embody all three qualities. They understand that leadership is stewardship, not entitlement. Protection is not about shielding people from discomfort, but ensuring that righteousness, fairness, and dignity guide every decision that shapes their environment.

In the workplace, protection should look like cultivating a safe and respectful environment, ensuring fairness and justice, and creating processes that guard people from mistreatment. It is the leader's responsibility to ensure that policies, decisions, and systems promote wellbeing rather than harm. Protection also means addressing toxic behaviors quickly, advocating for those without a voice, and reinforcing a culture where harassment, abuse, and favoritism have no place. Leaders who protect others do not merely correct problems; they prevent them by creating structures where people can work, grow, and belong without fear.

When leaders commit to protecting others, culture shifts. Fear is replaced with safety. Pressure gives way to integrity. People speak more openly, trust more deeply, and work more freely because they know their leader will not trade their wellbeing for convenience or public approval. Ethical leaders reflect the heart of Christ, who defends the weak and uplifts the forgotten. Their influence lasts because it is rooted in justice, mercy, and humility. The leader who protects others becomes a channel of God's character in the workplace, leaving a legacy defined not by position, but by the lives strengthened and safeguarded through their faithful leadership.

Weekly Practice in Faith

This week, reflect on areas where people rely on you for protection. It may be emotional support, ethical clarity, or advocacy in a difficult situation. Identify one specific way you can protect someone entrusted to your leadership. It could be slowing a process to ensure fairness, addressing a concern with care, or speaking up for someone whose voice is ignored.

Write down the action you intend to take and bring it before God in prayer. Protection does not always look dramatic. Sometimes it is a quiet decision that communicates, "You matter." Leaders who protect others reflect the heart of Christ, who came not to be served but to serve.

Time for Reflection

Micah 6:8 reminds leaders that ethical leadership balances justice, mercy, and humility. Acting justly requires standing for what is right. Loving mercy requires compassion when mistakes happen. Walking humbly requires remembering that leadership is a trust from God, not a platform for self centered influence.

Reflect on how these qualities show up in your leadership. Are your decisions fair? Do you respond with compassion when others fall short? Are you leading from humility or self protection? Ask God to help your leadership become a refuge, not a risk, for those under your care.

Weekly Prayer

Lord, thank You for showing me what is good. Teach me to act with justice, to love mercy, and to walk humbly before You. Give me courage to make ethical decisions that protect others, even when it is neither easy nor popular. Shape my leadership to reflect Your heart so that those I serve are strengthened and safeguarded. In Jesus' name, Amen.

WEEK 50

Ethical Leadership Comes at a Cost

"The one whose walk is blameless, who does what is righteous, who speaks the truth from their heart... who keeps an oath even when it hurts, and does not change their mind."

Psalm 15:2, 4 (NIV)

Ethical leadership often comes at a cost. Doing what is right can mean facing criticism, losing opportunities, fracturing relationships, or even standing alone. The temptation to compromise, bend the truth, or take a shortcut is always close by because those paths appear easier, safer, and more efficient. Yet Scripture reminds us that righteousness is never about convenience. It is about conviction. Psalm 15 paints a picture of the person who walks in integrity, who speaks truth from a sincere heart, and who keeps their word even when it is painful or unpopular.

In leadership, the price of doing what is right may include sacrificing popularity, profit, or personal comfort. These sacrifices are rarely glamorous. They are usually costly and quiet. But they build something far more enduring than short term results. They build trust, credibility, and a legacy of moral strength that can withstand pressure. Leaders who choose integrity over ease reflect Christ Himself, who paid the ultimate cost to redeem what was broken. This week challenges you to consider whether you are willing to uphold God's standards even when it costs you something you value.

Leadership Wisdom for the Christian Leader

Doing the right thing sounds noble until it becomes costly. Many leaders reach defining crossroads where the ethical choice is also the painful one. Opportunities may be lost, influence can shrink, relationships may strain, and criticism may follow. These are the moments that reveal what truly anchors a leader. Some trade conviction for convenience. Others choose the harder road and carry the weight of their decision alone. These costly decisions become the proving ground of character.

Psalm 15:2–4 highlights the kind of leader God honors, one who walks blamelessly, practices righteousness, speaks truth from the heart, and keeps an oath even when it hurts. This does not call for perfection. It calls for courage. Courage to refuse shortcuts. Courage to stand firm when pressured to compromise. Courage to remain faithful when the right decision is unpopular or misunderstood. Leaders who embody this kind of integrity know that righteousness is not defined by what they can get away with, but by what honors Christ and protects others.

Leaders who embrace the cost of doing what is right build influence that cannot be fabricated. Their teams learn to trust their word because it is consistent. Their decisions create stability because they are grounded in truth. God uses these leaders in ways visible and invisible, opening doors that character alone can unlock. The sacrifices of today become the seeds of tomorrow's credibility and spiritual authority. Ethical leadership may cost something in the moment, but it produces a harvest that outlasts every temporary loss.

Weekly Practice in Faith

This week, examine one decision you've been postponing because of the personal cost attached to it. Is there an ethical step you know you should take, but have hesitated to embrace? Bring that situation before God each morning. Ask for courage, clarity, and conviction. Then take one practical step toward doing what is right, even if discomfort comes with it. Let that step be an offering of obedience that honors God and strengthens your integrity.

Time for Reflection

Psalm 15 challenges leaders to embody righteousness both in public actions and private decisions. Integrity is not proven by the promises we make, but by the commitments we keep when keeping them is difficult. As you reflect this week, ask yourself: Are you willing to sacrifice what is easy for what is right? Ethical leadership may not always earn applause, but it earns something far greater, God's approval and the trust of those you serve.

Weekly Prayer

Lord, strengthen me to lead with integrity, to speak truthfully, and to honor every commitment that aligns with Your standards. When I am tempted to take shortcuts or protect my own interests, remind me of the eternal value of righteousness. Shape my decisions so they reflect Your character. Let every sacrifice be an act of worship. In Jesus' name, Amen.

Leadership and the Cross

THE LEGACY OF A LEADER

Weeks 51-52

As we begin this final section of the devotional journey, we turn our focus toward legacy; not just how we lead today, but the kind of influence we leave behind. These closing weeks invite you to pause, look back on the road you've traveled, and consider the mark your life and leadership have already made on others.

Legacy is not built in a single moment of success but through the steady accumulation of choices shaped by integrity, humility, and love. It reaches beyond what others see in the moment and takes root in hearts and places you may never witness.

Over the next two weeks, you'll be invited to write two letters. Each one offers space to reflect, release, and give thanks. Through these letters, you will capture what God has done in you, what He continues to grow through you, and what He will carry forward beyond you.

As you reflect on your journey, rest in the truth that the seeds you've planted through faith, courage, and quiet obedience will continue to grow in ways only God can bring to harvest.

WEEK 51

Leaving a Legacy that Matters

"The world and its desires pass away,

but whoever does the will of God lives forever."

1 John 2:17 (NIV)

Every lasting legacy requires a letting go. The world often tells leaders to hold tightly to power, success, and recognition; to build something impressive and keep their name attached to it. Yet Scripture reminds us that those pursuits eventually fade. What endures is not what we control, but what we surrender to God's purpose.

Leadership rooted in eternity looks different from leadership driven by ambition. It means leading with open hands, trusting that the influence we yield to God will outlive anything we build on our own. It is choosing to serve rather than strive, to obey rather than perform, and to seek God's approval more than the applause of others.

The cost of a lasting legacy is found in these quiet moments of obedience, when we forgive instead of retaliate, listen instead of defend, or stay steady when recognition never comes. These are the decisions that shape a leader's soul and tell the truer story of success.

Doing the will of God redefines leadership itself. It is no longer about being remembered, but about reflecting Him well. In the end, legacy is not measured by how much we achieve, but by how faithfully we followed when the world told us to do otherwise.

Weekly Practice in Faith

From the beginning, this devotional has invited you into moments of reflection and a spiritual journey as a leader who desires to lead as Christ taught us. This week, take a few moments to think about the kind of legacy you want your leadership to leave behind.

For this week's practice, write a letter of commitment to your future self as a reminder of what truly matters in leadership. Consider how you hope your influence will continue to make a difference after you have moved on. These may be qualities you have modeled, values you have upheld, or lessons you hope others will carry forward.

As you write, imagine you are speaking to the version of yourself who may be weary, uncertain, tempted to measure success by recognition or results, or easily swayed by outside voices. Encourage yourself to remain grounded in faith, steady in purpose, and confident in the quiet work God is doing through you.

Let this letter be a voice of wisdom from your present self, one that reminds you why you lead, who you serve, and what kind of legacy you hope to leave. Encourage yourself to stay faithful to the work that lasts; the work shaped by integrity, humility, and love. Remember that the most enduring influence often comes through quiet obedience and steady perseverance.

End your letter with a prayer of commitment, asking God to help you lead with a heart that seeks His will above everything else. When you are finished, fold the letter and keep it with your devotional as a personal reminder of the legacy you want your life to tell.

Letter of Commitment to Yourself

_____

_____

_____

A 52-Week Devotional for Leaders

Weekly Prayer

Lord, Teach me to build a legacy that honors You, not myself. Help me lead with humility, serve with love, and stay faithful when no one is watching. When I grow weary, remind me that what is done in Your name endures. May my influence reflect Your heart and draw others closer to You. Amen.

WEEK 52

The Seeds We Have Sown

"May the favor of the Lord our God rest on us; establish the work of our hands for us - yes, establish the work of our hands."

Psalm 112:6 (NIV)

You have reached the end of this devotional journey, but not the end of your influence as a leader. Over these weeks, you have reflected, prayed, surrendered, and served, not to build a legacy of your own name, but to lead as Christ led. Each step of obedience, each act of integrity, and each moment of grace has planted a seed that God continues to nurture.

Legacy is not measured by applause or accomplishment but by the quiet fruit that grows from faithfulness. You have sown seeds through your leadership: encouragement that lifted others, wisdom that guided them, and love that reflected Christ's heart. Some of those seeds you may already see sprouting, while others will grow in places and seasons beyond your sight.

Psalm 90 reminds us that it is God who establishes the work of our hands. The good you have done, the lives you have touched, and the truth you have shared all rest in His hands now. He is faithful to bring to harvest what you have planted in faith. Your leadership legacy lives on in every heart you have influenced toward hope, purpose, and grace.

Weekly Practice in Faith

Every leader leaves a trail of words spoken, actions taken, and lives influenced. These are the seeds you sow through your leadership. This 52-week journey has been grounded in Scripture and guided by the C.R.O.S.S. Leadership Model which consists of *Character, Responsibility, Obedience, Service, and Sacrifice.*

In the space provided, write to the version of yourself who began this journey 52 weeks ago. Reflect on how your *character* has grown through faith, how *responsibility* has deepened your influence, how *obedience* has strengthened your trust in God, how *service* has softened your heart toward others, and how *sacrifice* has taught you what it means to lead with love.

Celebrate the growth and renewal that have taken place in you. Thank God for the quiet strength He has built through your experiences, and for the seeds of faith and leadership that now live in the people you have served.

Weekly Prayer

Lord, Thank You for shaping my life and leadership through over the past 52 weeks. Continue to strengthen my character, guide my obedience, and keep my heart ready to serve and sacrifice for Your glory. Establish the work of my hands and let my legacy reflect Your love and truth. May all I have sown continue to grow in ways that honor You. Amen.

Leadership and the Cross

From the Author: A Prayer for the Journey Ahead

Thank you for walking through this devotional journey. Over these weeks, you have given God room to speak into your leadership, your purpose, and your faith. My hope is that these reflections have strengthened your confidence in Christ and helped you lead with greater humility, clarity, and trust in God's plan.

Though these pages come to a close, your leadership story continues. The growth God has begun in you will bear fruit as you keep choosing His way. Legacy does not end with the final devotion. It is built day by day through small acts of service, honest decisions, and leadership that reflects Jesus to the people who depend on you.

As you move forward, remember that your leadership matters because God has called you to it. Stay rooted in His Word. Seek His presence more than approval. Lead with courage even when the path feels uncertain. May every step reflect the One who leads you.

I close this journey with prayer:

Lord,
Thank You for guiding me through this season of reflection and growth. Strengthen the seeds You have planted in my heart and help me lead in ways that honor You. Keep my character pure, my focus steady, and my leadership faithful to Your standards. May every decision I make reflect Your love and bring You glory. Amen.

GLOSSARY

Accountability: The obligation to accept responsibility for one's actions and decisions, and to be answerable for the outcomes.

Affirmation: The action or process of providing emotional support or encouragement.

Character: The mental and moral qualities distinctive to an individual.

Conflict Management: The process of limiting the negative aspects of conflict while increasing the positive aspects.

Conviction: A firmly held belief or opinion.

Dignity: The state or quality of being worthy of honor or respect.

Emotional Intelligence: The ability to understand, use, and manage your own emotions in positive ways to relieve stress, communicate effectively, empathize with others, overcome challenges, and defuse conflict. (Goleman, 1995; Salovey & Mayer, 1990).

Empathy: The ability to understand and share the feelings of another.

Ethics: Moral principles that govern a person's behavior or the conducting of an activity.

Humility: A modest or low view of one's own importance; humbleness.

Integrity: The quality of being honest and having strong moral principles.

Leadership: The action of leading a group of people or an organization.

Motivation Theory: Theory which helps to explain what drives human behavior and the factors that compel people to work toward a specific goal. (Herzberg, Mausner, & Snyderman, 1959).

Obedience: Compliance with an order, request, or law or submission to another's authority.

Organizational Change: The process by which a company or organization alters its structure, strategies, or operational methods.

Responsibility: The state or fact of having a duty to deal with something or of having control over someone.

Sacrifice: An act of giving up something valued for the sake of something else regarded as more important or worthy.

Servant Leadership: A leadership philosophy in which the main goal of the leader is to serve. This is different from traditional leadership where the leader's main focus is to achieve goals for the organization. (Greenleaf, 1977).

Service: The action of helping or doing work for someone.

Situational Leadership: A leadership theory that suggests there is no single best way to lead; instead, the most effective leadership style is one that adapts to the readiness or maturity level of the individual or group. (Hersey & Blanchard, 1969).

Spiritual Leadership: A leadership style that involves the act of influencing, guiding, and nurturing others toward God's purposes, with an emphasis on servanthood and moral character.

Strategic Thinking: A mental or thinking process applied in the context of achieving a goal or set of goals in a game or other endeavor.

Teamwork: The collaborative effort of a group to achieve a common goal or to complete a task in the most effective and efficient way.

Transformational Leadership: A leadership style in which leaders encourage, inspire, and motivate employees to innovate and create change that will help grow and shape the future success of the company.

REFERENCES

Goleman, D. (1995). *Emotional intelligence: Why it can matter more than IQ*. Bantam Books.

Greenleaf, R. K. (1977). *Servant leadership: A journey into the nature of legitimate power and greatness*. Paulist Press.

Hersey, P., & Blanchard, K. H. (1969). Life cycle theory of leadership. Training and Development Journal, 23(5), 26–35.

Herzberg, F. I., Mausner, B., & Snyderman, B. (1959). *The motivation to work* (2nd ed.). New York: John Wiley.

Salovey, P., & Mayer, J. D. (1990). Emotional intelligence. *Imagination, Cognition and Personality*, 9(3), 185–211.

www.ingramcontent.com/pod-product-compliance
Lightning Source LLC
Chambersburg PA
CBHW050519100526
44581CB00001B/30